What Really Happened to Michael Jackson The King of Pop

The Evil Side of the Entertainment Industry

*Leonard Rowe tells
this story in his own words*

What Really Happened to Michael Jackson the King of Pop

Disclaimer:
The content of this book is solely the opinion and factual life experience of the author.

First Printing: November 2010

ISBN: 978-0-9827622-0-2

This book may also be purchased at
www.whatreallyhappenedtomj.com

Justice Reward Fund

A portion of the proceeds from the sale of this book will be set aside for a reward fund. This reward fund is for those who come forward with information that will lead to the prosecution and conviction of any person or persons other than Dr. Conrad Murray, that were involved in the conspiracy which led to the death of Michael Jackson.

If you have any information
Please contact
The US Department of Justice
(202) 514-2000

Table of Contents

Dedication

To the Fans of Michael Jackson

If Michael ever touched your heart, or moved you in any way; this book is dedicated to you, his beloved fans. Michael's fans were very important to him; he cherished them, and always thought of them before going on stage. The music he performed was often times dedicated to them, with songs like, "Heal The World," "Black or White," "You Are Not Alone," and "They Don't Really Care About Us," just to name a few.

I truly believe that Michael carried the weight of the world on his shoulders. He sincerely cared about "healing the world, and making it a better place." So, I dedicate this book to anyone who has ever been or still is a Michael Jackson fan. May his music and legacy always remind you that *we all* can do something to make a *change.*

In reading this book, I hope you will be given a rare glimpse into the life of Michael Jackson, and I truly hope you realize that he was just as remarkable off stage as he was on stage.

Few had the privilege to know him personally as I did; I know now what an honor and a blessing that was for me. I would like to say to all of Michael's fans around the world that Michael truly loved you all. And always cared about what you thought about him.

It comes to mind, when I once asked him as he was about to perform, not to exert himself so much on stage, because he was ill at the time. He looked directly at me and said, "I can't do that, I can't do the people that way, I must give them (the fans) all that I have." This is how he *truly* felt about you, *his fans.*

So I dedicate this book to you. *The most loyal and beloved fans in the world. The fans of Michael Jackson, "The True King of Pop."*

Acknowledgement

I would like to take this opportunity to acknowledge and give thanks to three legendary concert promoters that paved the way for so many to follow in the concert promotion industry. They have received little or no recognition for their accomplishments. During their careers they never received the right to work in a non discriminatory environment. But yet they still somehow prevailed and prospered.

Henry Winn

Born in the year of 1920 in Albany Georgia. He started his concert promoting career in the early 1960's. He was one of the most respected Concert Promoters ever to engage in the business of concert promoting. He was responsible for the success of other promoters such as Teddy Powell, from Newark New Jersey, R. J. Russo from Houston Texas, Agnew of Regal Sports in St. Louis, Missouri, and many more. He promoted and toured such artists as James Brown, B.B. King, The Drifters, Jerry Butler, Aretha Franklin, Otis Redding, The Temptations, and Sam Cooke, just to mention a few. He was known and respected for his impeccable character and integrity. He was truly viewed as, and still remains, a legend in the concert promotion Industry. He always believed that prosperity should always be shared among all of his associates. I will always remember something that he said. "It doesn't make me look like a hell of a guy if I'm the only one with money. It gives us more power as a group if all of us share in the wealth." He passed away February 13th, 1976 in Lexington, Kentucky.

Teddy Powell

Teddy Powell was born in Lumberton, N.C. in or around the year 1920. He later moved to Newark, New Jersey where he became interested in the entertainment industry. He began his concert promoting career in the mid 1940's, promoting such artists as Louis Jordan, The Platters, Brook Benton, Nat King Cole, The Drifters, Muddy Waters, The Ink Spots, Etta James and Sam Cooke. His Concert Promoting career spanned over a half a century. He was known to other Concert Promoters as the "Grandfather of concert promoting". In the '60's and '70's he toured such artists as Sly and The Family Stone, The Parliament Funkadelic, The Temptations, Graham Central Station, Nancy Wilson, Jerry Butler, Al Green, and The O'Jays.

He was often known and recognized for his unique laughter, and for referring to everyone as "Homes". His favorite greeting was "What's up Homes?" Teddy was and still remains a legendary figure in the Concert Promotion industry. He paved the way for newcomers such as myself and many others. He passed away in Newark, New Jersey in the early '90's.

Louis Grey

Louis Grey was born in Little Rock, Arkansas on December 28th, 1936. At the age of ten his family moved to Kansas City, Missouri, where he stayed until the age of 27. In 1963 he uprooted from Kansas City and moved to Los Angeles, California. This is when he discovered that he had the talent to become a concert promoter. He then opened the doors to his concert promotion company, Worldwide Productions, and began his career as a concert promoter. His first big break came when the Godfather of Soul, James Brown gave him the opportunity to promote his show. It was a huge success. Years later he changed the name of his company to Louis Grey Productions and became a force in the concert promotion industry. He went on to promote national tours with such legendary artists as The O'Jays, The Temptations, Earth Wind & Fire, Stevie Wonder, Marvin Gaye, and many, many more. Louis Grey was my colleague and friend. He died in April 1990 in Los Angeles, California. He was truly a legend in the concert promotion industry.

Introduction

From where I sit today it's been nine long months since Michael Jackson passed away. He was pronounced dead at 2:26 p.m. (PST) on June 25th, 2009. As long as I live I will never forget where I was, or how I felt when I heard the news that a very dear and close friend and a person that I loved was gone forever. To all of you he may have been The King of Pop or a music legend, and he was in every sense of the word. But to *me,* he was my *friend*, and a person I owe a great deal of gratitude to. The events that lead to his untimely death still haunt me to this day. I'm not writing this book in hopes of seeking revenge. I simply want to tell the truth about what really happened to the legend known around the world as Michael Jackson, The King of Pop. For if I didn't write this, I fear my life would be filled with regret. The world loved Michael, and it's for him and the sake of his memory that I must make this endeavor.

The day Michael passed away started out like any other for me. I had only been home from Los Angeles for a few days. Prior to that, I had been working with Michael in LA. Now I wonder if I hadn't come home maybe I could have done something that would have caused him to still be alive. As I drove through the busy streets of Atlanta, I relished in the brief comfort of being home, fully knowing I was due to fly back to Los Angeles the next day. Michael was preparing for the London tour, and I was trying my best to do what he had asked me to do; watch over his business affairs, and AEG the Concert Promotion Company, he had contracted with to do the London shows. I was also trying my best to fight what I perceived to be the evil that was surrounding him at that time. There were several suspicious things that had transpired, things that had Michael and I both concerned and puzzled.

I received a call from Randy Jackson (Michael's youngest brother) around 3:30 p.m. (EST). As soon as I answered, Randy said, "The paramedics have just taken Michael to UCLA

Hospital." "*Go to the hospital, call me once you get there, and let me know what's going on,*" I said, as I made a beeline to my house. By this point my mind was racing, wondering what was really happening. The initial thought I had was that Michael was pulling a prank or faking it. I knew that he did not want to do the London dates nor was he in any physical condition to do them. I thought this was his way of getting out of it. A few minutes later Randy called again and informed me that the media had announced that Michael was dead. I kept driving, but my heart and my mind were both racing. "*What is going on?*" I kept thinking.

In my mind I could see Michael, and I couldn't get past the nagging feeling that something was terribly wrong. *How could Michael be dead?* Sure, he wasn't in the best physical shape, but I certainly didn't think he had one foot in the grave.

Once I returned home, Randy called me again and confirmed that Michael was gone. Disbelief, confusion, and unspeakable grief consumed me in that instant. I asked Randy where was his mother Katherine. He told me she was there at the hospital. I said I would call her in a few minutes. Later I called her, and she picked up the phone. I could hear the turmoil in her voice. I asked her, "*When do you think I should come?*" Katherine replied, "*I think you should come now.*"

So, I packed and left immediately the next morning. On my flight over, I kept thinking of all the things that Michael and I had discussed privately. All of the suspicious activities that had transpired months and weeks prior to his death played out in my mind over and over again. People that Michael vowed to never do business with again such as John Branca and Frank DiLeo had suddenly been brought back into his life by Randy Phillips of AEG. Michael and I could never figure out why. We discussed this on many occasions, and now that I can put it all together, I can see everything so clearly. At that time, we were never sure about John Branca, Michael's former attorney, whom Michael had many problems with in the past that had cost him millions of dollars. But we had an idea about Frank DiLeo, Michael's former manager. We strongly believed that Frank DiLeo was being brought back into the picture by Randy Phillips because of me. I was the only person around Michael that AEG and Randy Phillips did not control financially, and Randy Phillips, having known me for a few years, knew that I would possibly create a problem for him if he was not working in Michael Jackson's best interest. I know now that he clearly wasn't. I can see now that I was going to interfere with their plans.

These suspicious activities have propelled me to write this book, to tell the world what is being hidden by the media and the powers that be in the entertainment industry. A great injustice is being played out daily, and I'm here to set the record straight. Michael Jackson, The King of Pop, in my opinion was murdered, and his words still haunt me to this day: *"They want my catalogue (music publishing rights) Rowe and they will kill me for it."* Few know this, but Michael owned fifty percent of Sony's entire music catalogue. He never wanted to sell; he wanted to keep it for his children. The powers that be, knew that Michael and The Michael Jackson name was worth billions and billions of dollars, and he was worth more to them dead than alive. With him dead they would be able to move in and control the wealth that his name and his brand would bring for years and years to come. In my opinion, that is exactly what they are doing today with the benefit of a phony and fraudulent will. The powers that be, have been trying to keep me quiet by committing slander against me, and trying to prevent me from doing interviews on the talk show circuit. I must confess, I am not one to be intimidated easily or one who will back down. Michael can't speak now, but I can...*and I will.*

This story is a story that must be told. The public as well as Michael's millions of fans deserve the right to know what really happened to him. Michael may have been a Jackson, but he belonged to the world. This story is laced with discriminatory treatment towards African Americans and minorities in the entertainment industry. AEG had a contract with Michael that was in my opinion nothing less than a cocked financial gun pointed to his head.

I truly believe he was being totally exploited. This is a true account of what really happened to Michael Jackson, and an up close look at the evil side of the entertainment industry.

TO ALL READERS
BRACE YOURSELF!!!

CHAPTER ONE

WHEN I FIRST MET
MICHAEL JACKSON

Michael Jackson & Leonard Rowe
Summer of 1979, Los Angeles, CA

When I First Met Michael Jackson

For you to understand what really happened to Michael, I need to take you back a few years. At the age of twenty-three in the year 1974, I became interested in the entertainment industry. At that particular juncture in my life, I thought this would be a wonderful industry for someone to build a career. But I also knew it would not be easy for me, there would be many stumbling blocks that would lie ahead for a young African American from Columbus, a small town in Georgia, who had no connections or financial backing. It was only by the grace of Almighty God and a helping hand along the way (which I will discuss later) that I was able to make that entry.

For all of my adult life, I have been a concert promoter. Concert promoters are a rare breed of human beings. I would go so far as to say that it is imperative for one to possess street smarts or common sense as we may call it, along with an upper mid-level education, and an above average shrewdness wouldn't hurt either.

I had the honor and privilege of meeting Michael in February of 1979. I flew out to Chicago to speak to his father Joe Jackson about a few concert dates for his sons, The Jacksons, who had faded from the charts in recent years. We all gathered in one of their hotel rooms for a brief meeting. Still to this day, I can remember, the first time I met Michael; I immediately noticed something different about him. There was something in his eyes; it was like being in the presence of someone holy. He had a different spirit about him, and I knew at that point he was someone special. There was something that he had that I immediately knew very few people possessed. Later it came as no surprise to me when his career excelled and he became a sensation around the world. Shortly after that first initial meeting, The Jacksons went on a ten date concert tour that was booked by their agency which at the time was Regency Artists. I promoted five of the ten shows. It was during this time that my relationship with the Jackson family began to flourish.

One show I remember in particular was in Jacksonville, Florida, at the Jacksonville Coliseum. As I watched The Jacksons on stage, I noticed how incredibly talented they were. They literally thrilled the capacity crowd of over 10,000 people. The Jacksons performed like they had been doing this all their lives, and in fact they had. But I knew there was something missing. They didn't have the production, wardrobe, and publicity their superb performance deserved. A few weeks later I flew out to California to visit them at their home. There I presented to them a proposal and a plan to do a fifty city concert tour; and to revamp their entire act. After a lengthy discussion, they loved the idea and decided to give me the exclusive rights to promote their entire tour.

From that point my relationship with Michael and his brothers continued to grow. Once Michael began to know you and felt he could trust you, he would talk you to death...he would talk about everything. He revealed to me on numerous occasions how deep he was, and how his thinking and wisdom were well beyond his years. I remember on one such occasion we were discussing his brother Jermaine leaving the group and staying with Motown Records. Michael asked me what I thought of Berry Gordy (owner of Motown Records.) I told him I thought he was a good business-minded person; he said, "I do too." He then looked me in the eye and said, "I love Berry Gordy. I wanted to stay at Motown, as Jermaine did, but I knew I couldn't stay. I knew my family could not survive without me." That statement told me a lot about Michael Jackson. He carried the weight of the world on his shoulders most of his life and never complained.

Several weeks before going on tour, we would have meeting after meeting at their Encino, CA home each week. At the end of every meeting Michael would follow me to my car for a one-on-one conversation, and every time he would tell me about this new album he had coming out. He would say, "Rowe, I have this new album coming, it will be out in a few weeks and it may help us out on tour."

He had never made a solo album before, and to be honest I really didn't pay much attention to him. I was mainly concerned with the tour, and the album The Jacksons had out at the time called "Destiny." I figured this album would be good enough for us to do well.

For the next few weeks, the same thing would occur time and time again after each meeting. Michael would walk me out to my car, and he would say, "Rowe, don't forget about my album that is coming out." I would uninterestedly say, "Yes, Michael, okay."

About two weeks before tickets went on sale for the tour, he walked me out to my car again, and as he looked around to see if anyone was looking, he pulled out from under his jacket the cover of his new album. It had a picture of him wearing a tuxedo and studded socks, and the title of it was "Off the Wall." Still uninterested, I said, "That looks nice, Michael." A couple of weeks later the album was released. The first single to be released was, "Don't Stop Till You Get Enough." The song went straight to number one and so did the album, shattering every record in the recording industry. Our ticket sales went through the roof.

It was because of that album; we sold out forty-eight of the

Rowe engaging in conversation with The Jacksons in August 1979, before leaving L.A. to begin the "Off The Wall Tour".

fifty concerts and broke Elvis Presley's record in seventeen cities. By this time I was pretty excited, but Michael had a very calm demeanor, like he expected it to happen all along. Occasionally while we were on tour, I would go to his room after the show to make sure he was happy with the job we were doing. I always noticed that beside him on his bed there would always be an open Bible that he was reading. One night in particular, we were in Cleveland, Ohio, and as I was entering his hotel room, he returned to his bed. He then looked at me and said, "Rowe, we are doing very well, aren't we?" I said in return, "Mike, we are doing very, very well."

The morning we were scheduled to leave Los Angeles to begin the tour I had a conversation with Joe, Michael's father, and I will never forget that conversation. He was angry with me because I had hired a very expensive wardrobe designer by the name of Bill Witten to design and make the boys' costumes. His cost was over $200,000. We had also brought in an elaborate and expensive production company. We also hired two PR firms to cover the entire tour. Our total cost was well into the hundreds of thousands per week. This was a lot of money in those days. But I felt that the boys needed this to propel them to the status where I felt they should be.

Joe's words to me were, "Rowe, when you get out on the road and you can't pay these bills, don't call me. You could have gotten the same person who used to design the boys' wardrobe for a lot cheaper, around three hundred dollars per man. That lady has been doing their wardrobe for years. Don't call me when you run into trouble."

I must admit on the inside I was scared, but I couldn't show it. I assured him we would be fine. We left LA and Joe stayed behind. Michael and his brothers had put a lot of trust in me, and I had to deliver. I prayed daily that God would be with me, directing and guiding me. I will always believe that He did.

The Jacksons had rehearsed for months; they were like a well polished machine. There was no group in the world better than The Jacksons. Our ticket sales had made us the top selling tour for that year. Halfway through the tour after about twenty-four dates, Michael became very ill from an infection in his throat that had spread to his ear. I had a special doctor fly in from Las Vegas hoping he could perform a miracle that would keep Michael going.

Once the doctor examined him, he told us both that Michael was in bad shape. Michael looked at me and asked with a very weak voice, "Rowe how many shows do we have left?" As bad as I hated to say it, I told him we had about twenty-five shows left. I said to him that we were at the half way point of the tour. He knew that I had everything that I owned and could borrow on the line. He saw how worried I was. He stared at me; then said in the strangest voice, "Don't worry Rowe, I'll make it." We had two more shows to do, Atlanta, Georgia, and Mobile, Alabama, before we had a ten day break. After that we were due to play Honolulu, Hawaii. It was a grueling pace.

Michael was singing sixteen to eighteen songs per night. Michael came out of his dressing room in Mobile, to go on stage. This was the last show before the break. I noticed he looked very weak; he did not look well at all, he could barely speak. Concerned about his health, I said to him, "Mike, don't overexert yourself tonight. Don't do all of the dancing and spinning, just sing and try to get through the show." Michael looked at me and said, "Rowe, I can't do that. I can't do the people that way. I must give them all I have."

I knew at that moment what type of person was in my midst. I watched him while he was on the stage that night, and he truly was giving it all he had. When the performance was over, he had to be carried away.

Michael flew home to California for a few days and rejuvenated himself. Meanwhile, his album, "Off The Wall," was shattering every record in the music industry, with twenty million copies sold. Looking back on that time, what Michael was doing was truly remarkable, as this was even before the time that music videos existed. Michael told me just before he died that he always thought "Off The Wall" was his best album ever.

During the tour we were constantly battling the evils of the entertainment industry. I was the first African American concert

Michael Jackson & Leonard Rowe
Celebrating after the show in L.A. in December 1979,
at the world famous Chasen's restaurant.

promoter that had ever toured The Jacksons, or that ever had a close relationship with the family. The powers of the industry hated that relationship. In fact, they hate any relationship between a black concert promoter and what they call "a crossover superstar artist." A crossover artist is an artist that appeals to both black and white audiences.

As long as they could keep these relationships from existing, they could control not only that artist, but the entire entertainment industry as well. Controlling the industry and the destiny of all involved has been and still remains very lucrative for the booking agencies, and people that control the music industry. They are able to control the future of all artists, the venues in which they play, and the promoters for whom they work, as well as the talent cost and ticket prices.

In the mid 1980's, record albums and tapes by Michael Jackson, Prince, and Lionel Richie accounted for the sales of close to forty million copies in the United States alone. Surely this is an indication of the importance of blacks in the music and entertainment industry. Once these and other African American artists reach this type of popularity, the ticket selling power for their concerts becomes enormous. At this stage in the game, unknowingly to the general public, they are taken away from black concert promoters and the black business communities and given to the white concert promoters to reap enormous profits. The use of a black concert promoter has always served as the financial bridge for that concert dollar to return to the black community.

Black concert promoters are more likely to use other black businesses such as production, catering, printing, limousine services, tour accountants, and to advertise and promote their concerts through black-owned media outlets. To protect themselves, these ruthless booking agencies say that there are

**Marlon, Michael, Tito & Rowe
taking a walk in the park in LA (1979).**

very few black concert promoters if any, which can come up with the deposits and guarantees needed to promote their artist.

They first deny us the right to work and build our businesses and later say we don't have any money. This is equivalent to denying a person the right to an education, yet later complaining of their ignorance. Black concert promoters and the black business community are put in a "catch-twenty-two" situation by this industry.

After the tour with The Jacksons, Michael's career was soaring, however, the powers of the entertainment industry now saw me as a threat, and immediately I was "blackballed". None of the major agencies would do business with me. I truly believe this was being implemented and orchestrated by Richard Rosenburg and his crew from Regency Artists, The Jacksons former booking agency; who were now in power at The William Morris Agency.

In the mid 80's, I started speaking out about the discriminatory treatment towards blacks and minorities in the concert promotion industry. Whenever blacks and minorities have spoken out, complained, or acted against the unfair and/or prejudiced practices of the industry, they have always been "blackballed". Come to think of it, I suppose that is why this type of conspiratorial treatment is referred to as "blackballed". I won't call any names, but blacks have been among those "blackballed" for generations.

Whenever you see a successful or well-known African American performer disappear off the face of the earth, the majority of the time they have been "blackballed". We must speak out against racism and discrimination whenever it rears its ugly head, but once we do we're "blackballed". Even if an African American in the music industry suggests that Whites are getting favorable treatment and proves it, nine out of ten times they are going to be "blackballed". Just try to make a suggestion that blacks should have more involvement in the touring aspect of other black entertainers, and most of the time you will be "blackballed". When this occurs, artists find themselves losing record deals as well as other money-making opportunities. The powers of this industry use whatever means possible from their relationships and connections in television, newspapers, the internet, as well as all other media outlets to falsely sabotage and assassinate your character. They are successful most of the time in killing your career. They like to throw rocks and hide their hands. It's truly a "go along and you will get along" system.

I consider myself the poster boy for "blackballing" by this industry. I have always felt the calling to rattle the cage or speak out against unfair and unjust treatment. After my confrontations with Richard Rosenberg, Peter Grosslight, and

Don Fischell, top executives of The Jacksons booking agency in 1979 and 1980 when I promoted their national tour, I became a victim of the "blackball" conspiracy. Whenever there's a concert tour of this magnitude, there's the potential for huge profits to be made. They always want to control these profits by any means necessary, no matter if the entertainer is black or white. Whenever they see or feel that a relationship between a high profile black artist and a black concert promoter is developing, they will do everything within their power to destroy that relationship. Where no problems exist, they will always seize the opportunity to create some, so they can destroy that relationship. They don't feel that black people have a right to control this type of revenue or wealth. Although the entertainer may be black and thousands of black people are the ones patronizing these shows, they still want to control all of the money.

By the time 1984 rolled around Michael's career was on the fast track, but I was experiencing problems in my own. After being "blackballed" and shut out of the industry, I was finding it really hard to survive and to support my family and business.

One day, I received a call from a concert promoter named Alan Haymon, who lived in Boston, that I had a lot of admiration for. I hadn't spoken to him in several years. We had become friends during The Jacksons tour. When I first met Haymon, he was a young struggling concert promoter attending Harvard University, and trying to get started in the music industry.

Back in 1979, he called and asked me if I would work with him when I came up to the New England area. I had received several calls in the past from other concert promoters both black and white that lived in that part of the country that wanted to work with us. But I really liked Haymon for some strange reason. I think it was because he was closer to my age than the other concert promoters, as we were both in our early to mid-twenties. As I look back now, I think fate was taking its course. I agreed to work with him over all the others. Back in those days when you were a tour promoter and you would work with a local concert promoter, the tour promoter's job was to bring the show in. I gave Haymon five markets, Syracuse, Rochester and Buffalo, New York along with Boston and Springfield, Massachusetts. His job was to advertise all five cities.

After I gave him the shows, I received a call from him a few days later. He said to me that he didn't have enough money to advertise all the cities that I had given him, but he had enough to advertise two of them. He told me I could take the rest, and give them to someone else if I wanted to and he would understand. But he said he wanted to be truthful with me. Haymon also said he could borrow the money from someone else, but he didn't want to do that because that would be involving someone else in my business.

At that particular time in my life, money was not an issue. As he was talking to me, I remembered when I was trying to get started myself, and how a promoter out of Detroit, Michigan, had treated me. I remembered how this promoter talked to me and the awful way he made me feel. I called this promoter one day at his office and introduced myself. This promoter was doing very well at the time. I asked him if I could buy a show from him for Columbus, Georgia, when he was touring. And I expressed to him how grateful I would be if he would allow me to do so. In a very arrogant tone he asked, "How did you get my number?" and hung up on me. Remembering that, I told Haymon not to worry. I asked him to go and place the ads in all of the cities, to call my office and speak to my assistant, Wanda Fields, and we would mail the checks, and pay all of the adverting bills. I assured him we would still be partners, and we would split everything fifty-fifty. I then said to him "I will cover it all." I'll never forget his response when he said, "For real, Rowe?"And I said, "For real."

Little did I know that small act of kindness would later benefit me enormously at a time when I really needed it. I said all of that to say this; in 1984, I received a call from Haymon. He was doing very well. He had just completed a very successful national tour with the late artist Rick James. He said, "I need to see you." He then came to Georgia, found me, and said, "Let's go to work!" I told him my finances were messed up at the time and I had no money, but before I could say anything further, he said, "Don't worry about that, Rowe. You don't need any money. We are going to do a tour for The Soft Sheen Hair Care Company out of Chicago. Once we get the proceeds from that, we will roll that over and promote the Budweiser Superfest." He looked at me again and said, "Rowe, you don't need any money". He then spoke the same words I had once spoken to him, "I will cover it all; let's go to work." Every time I speak of this I become teary-eyed. He literally carried me on his back until I was able to carry myself.

As long as I live, I will never forget what he did for me. During my darkest of days, he brought me light. After that Haymon and I spent fifteen years promoting The Budweiser Superfest and other shows around the nation together. Finally, I became stable again, and was able to take care of my business and employees. There will always be love and gratitude in my heart for my friend, Alan Haymon.

CHAPTER TWO

DOUBLE STANDARDS IN THE INDUSTRY

Double Standards in the Industry

In the year of 1996, I was elected President of the Black Promoters Association (BPA). This association was formed and established to bring equality and fairness for African American Promoters, in the concert promotion industry.

It was a typical sunny July morning; I woke up in my suburban Atlanta home and laid there in bed thinking. Something was weighing heavily on my mind. Business had been slow, very slow. I couldn't help but think about my future and the future of other black concert promoters. It might have been a sunny morning, but our future was looking dim to say the least. And I knew exactly why our situation had gotten so dim. It appeared to me that the major booking agencies in this country such as Creative Artists Agency (CAA), The William Morris Agency and The Howard Rose Agency (among others) were trying to make black concert promoters extinct!

I got up that morning, got dressed, and as I drove to my office on I-285, I was truly convinced that something sinister was being done to us by these agencies. I was scrambling to find work, and the other black concert promoters were also scrambling to find work, but no one was talking about it. Like any other day, I began calling the other black concert promoters. But this time I wasn't just talking about concerts, I was asking them if they were aware of what was going on. I had a lot of respect for these guys, but they couldn't see it. I saw a scary pattern that was only happening to black concert promoters. Once I realized what was happening, I started looking at the industry very carefully. I detected that the black concert promoters were not being allowed to profit in the industry.

What was very noticeable was that white concert promoters that had started with us during the same time period were all flourishing. Virtually all of them had become financially sound. I couldn't help but ask myself some questions. "What is causing the disparity?" "Are they better men than we are?" Every time I asked, the answer that would always return was "No." Being a black man in America I couldn't help but ask the next question. "Are they treated differently by the powers that control the entertainment industry?" The powers being, CAA, The William Morris Agency, The Howard Rose Agency, and other booking agencies. The answer that always returned was "Yes."

Like most of my colleagues, I had dedicated my entire adult life to the entertainment industry as a concert promoter. From the age of twenty-four up to the present, all I'd ever done was live, think, eat, and sleep the concert promotion business. For that entire length of time, I had witnessed the civil rights of blacks and minorities being totally violated.

I remember one time during the 90's I asked a booking agency for a date on Madonna in any city I could get her. I knew she would sell every ticket available no matter what city. They laughed. They told me she was working for the same concert promoters that she had always worked for.

There were two sets of rules -- one set of rules for white concert promoters and one set of rules for us, the black concert promoters. From the time I came into this business in 1975, I immediately saw something sinister. Black concert promoters couldn't promote white artists, but white concert promoters could promote any artist, black or white. This policy was in effect then, and believe it or not, even with a Black President in The White House it is still in effect now. The white concert promoters were flourishing because the talent and booking agencies would take the black artists from the black concert promoters once they reached what is called "crossover" status. The white concert promoters were doing all the white shows and the most profitable black shows too. It didn't take a rocket scientist to know that something was wrong with this equation. I have often said that when the powers of this industry are behind closed doors, they must say we are a group of stupid people, because we allow them to do to us what they would never allow anyone to do to them.

For instance, in the early 70's Lionel Richie and The Commodores first started together out of Tuskegee, Alabama. Before white concert promoters knew what a Commodore was, black concert promoters were the ones that promoted and nurtured them. We promoted them nationally and helped to launch their successful careers. After leaving The Commodores, Lionel Richie became a "crossover artist" and also became a client of The Howard Rose Agency. He then was taken away from black concert promoters and given to white concert promoters to reap the benefits of his successful career. No white artist in history has ever been taken away from white concert promoters and the white community and then given to black concert promoters and the black community to enjoy or reap the profits of their success.

Let's take Barbara Streisand for example, a white Jewish entertainer. If she decided that she was going to betray her own race of people, tour for black concert promoters, and allow the black community to profit from her success, she wouldn't only be "blackballed", we would probably find her in a ditch somewhere soon after this decision was made. But she would never commit to such a betrayal. Black entertainers seem to think its okay to do this, even though they never see this type of betrayal by any other race of people but their own. I have said many times that until this industry decides to do business without regard to one's race or religion, black people as a whole must wake up and stop this exploitation.

I will always have love and the highest level of respect and admiration for the legendary singing group The Isley Brothers. This group has been in existence for a half a century. During this time they have sold millions and millions of records, but have never received the recognition that they should have. That is because they have always refused to allow themselves to be owned, controlled, or manipulated by the powers of the entertainment industry. We should all applaud The Isley Brothers.

By the early 90's, black concert promoters were getting only a few black shows. I have always felt that the injustice in this business comes from the dominance, control, and conspiracy orchestrated mainly by CAA and The William Morris Agency. I strongly believe that these companies discriminate and violate the civil rights of many Americans as they see fit, simply because of their race.

Most people don't realize that the concert promotion industry remains one of the few long-standing segregated industries in our nation. Unlike other industries where the various parts of that industry form a well-integrated structure, the booking agency industry does not. This is the only industry where "the Jim Crow law" still exists. I have always noticed that blacks and minorities working at CAA and The William Morris Agency are grossly under represented at the professional and managerial levels. They are rarely equitably employed and never given positions of power or authority. These agencies may have a black person in the mailroom or a black agent, but that agent can only book black artists. I have never known of a black agent that booked white artists at CAA, The William Morris Agency or The Howard Rose Agency. Blacks are not put in these positions for obvious reasons by these agencies. Black concert promoters aren't given the opportunity by these agencies to enter into any type of contractual agreement to promote concerts featuring white artists. This has been the status quo for African Americans and minorities in the concert promotion industry for decades, *no exceptions made!* During my days in school, I was taught that in pursuing your goals in life you were able to go as far as your work ethic and dreams would allow. This is not true if you are an African American in the concert promotion industry.

By the 90's, while other aspects of American life had moved past this type of racist behavior, the entertainment industry had not. In this great country of ours, you have the right to choose your business, but as a business owner you do not have a right to choose the color of people you do business with. CAA, The William Morris Agency, The Howard Rose Agency, and other booking agencies have always ignored this fact. They still operate by the discriminatory and segregationist policies of the past. These types of injustices and civil rights violations have continued to fester in recent years.

Racism of this type has become more sophisticated, but it is no different than what I saw growing up in the South. No other industry in America so openly operates on such a racial level as this one. Let's take the real estate business. Years ago, when black people wanted to purchase a home and the realtor only showed them houses in black neighborhoods, the federal government intervened and called it "redlining." But that's exactly what the booking agencies did then and still do now. If I or any black concert promoter called CAA, The William Morris Agency, or any of the top booking agencies and asked for an artist for any given date, the booking agent would go down his or her black artist roster and read every name that was available for that date. What they won't do is go down the white artist roster and give us the availability of the white artists that are also available for that date. This is also "redlining." To put it simply, this is also discrimination.

My friends listen to me and listen to me carefully; do not be deceived. I have seen unusually deceptive tactics used by CAA and The William Morris Agency. They will go to great lengths to hide and camouflage their racism and discrimination. But make no mistake about it and do not be fooled. Racism is woven and embedded in the practices and policies of these agencies.

In my opinion, having evaluated what I have observed over the past thirty-five years, it's my belief that these booking agencies and white concert promoters also operate an illegal conspiracy in the concert promotion industry of America. Each major market in the United States is controlled essentially by one primary promoter. That promoter has always been of the white race. Simply stated by Alex Cooley, a white concert promoter located in Atlanta, "What we have is a 'good ole boys' network."

These agencies have never allowed a black person to be a part of this exclusive "good ole boys" conspiracy network. Blacks are never trusted to that degree by these agencies. These white concert promoters and their identities are well known among all the major booking agencies. When a white artist or a high profile black artist is represented by CAA, The William Morris Agency, or The Howard Rose Agency and wants to go on a national tour or stage a concert, there is no competitive bidding process. These agents book these dates and tours with the dominant concert promoter in that market. The relationships between these booking agencies and the dominant concert promoter in each region are virtually unbreakable.

This industry is dominated, controlled, and monopolized by a handful of giant booking agencies, namely CAA and The William Morris Agency. I have never seen any sensitivity or interest in fairness for black concert promoters or the black business communities come from these agencies. They have always operated virtually free of federal regulations, government intervention, or public pressure. These powerful booking agencies believe that because this type of racism in the music industry has existed for so many years, it should still be okay for it to continue to exist now. I think they believe that as long as they can keep it hidden, it's fine to discriminate and to ignore the current civil rights laws of this country. I can't help but ask myself why our government refuses to look this way or to assign the justice department to oversee this corruption filled industry.

These agencies have kept their corrupt practices silent through their intimidation. This corruption and conspiracy has been maintained by fear. There is always the fear of one losing any prospect of a future in the entertainment industry, so most people think it's best to keep silent. These agencies also make annual contributions to civil rights organizations such as The Urban League, NAACP, and The Martin Luther King Center. This is done to camouflage their discrimination and to keep them off the civil rights organization hit list. By receiving sizeable donations, I believe these organizations are most likely to ignore the wrongdoings of these talent and booking agencies.

Now that the situation was very clear to me, I had to do something. Later that year in the fall of 1996, I called for a meeting to be held in Atlanta. About ten of us from all over the country met to discuss the problems we were all facing as black concert promoters. About three or four of them had already gone out of business and were no longer promoting. It was a serious time for us. We were desperate. I didn't know what to do or say at that time, but I did know one thing, something had to be done and done fast if we were going to survive. Some black concert promoters had lost their homes, their families, and their businesses. I understood because one of the most painful situations I have had to experience over the years was the laying off of my own employees who were like family to me. This lay-off happened solely because we were being denied equal opportunity by the top booking agencies in America, namely CAA, The William Morris Agency, and The Howard Rose Agency. We weren't allowed to promote certain concerts solely because of our race.

At that very same meeting, I was elected as president of the Black Promoters Association (BPA). This organization was started to promote the interests of black promoters, to open the industry to free competition, and to eliminate racial discrimination. We all felt that this organization was very much needed at that time. The powerful booking agencies hated this organization because it showed togetherness on our part and gave us strength. They wanted to make sure that we always stayed divided. These agencies never wanted black concert promoters to be friends or to show any type of camaraderie. The way they did this was by keeping us at odds with one another. How it's done is by selling a black concert promoter out of Washington, D.C., a show in Atlanta where another black concert promoter lived and worked, and then giving the Atlanta promoter a show in Detroit where another black concert promoter lived and worked. This caused resentment among each other. For years we all knew they were playing us against each other, but the industry kept us so financially strained that it was hard to turn these shows down. White concert promoters were given a monopoly in their markets. They owned the unspoken right to that territory – no if, ands, or buts about it. The industry didn't allow any intervention between the white concert promoters. It was very clever what they were doing.

These agencies operate like in the days of organized crime when the mob controlled garbage collection and construction, among other industries. They did not need nor did they solicit competition; they were able to raise prices as they saw fit. Competition is never welcomed in an industry that is being controlled by an entity or totally dominated by a syndicate of people.

Our meeting had been a long time coming. Before it was over, I stood before everyone and gave my solemn promise to do everything within my power to better our situation. I told them that I would work diligently to fight the injustice and discrimination that we all had faced for so many years. We decided that we were going to stand up and collectively fight this corruption, collusion, and racial discrimination together.

About this same time, in the fall of 1996, we learned that recording star Toni Braxton was planning to tour with the highly successful artist, Kenny G. I had joined with Al Haymon to promote Toni Braxton the previous year on a tour with Frankie Beverly. Now she had become a huge success and was now being booked by The William Morris Agency. As always, she was being taken away from us, as other black artists had been in the past, after reaching star status, and given to the white concert promoters. I felt that the black concert promoters should have received the same opportunity to be involved again as white concert promoters were given when they had previously promoted an artist. This was the norm in the industry with white concert promoters. I knew there would be a problem. The headline artist, Kenny G, a White artist who was booked by CAA, was also on the bill. Therefore, neither Haymon nor I received a call concerning the tour. CAA was the agency in charge of booking the tour.

I decided to call CAA and inquire why black concert promoters were excluded from participation. The person that was head of the music department, Rob Light, and the responsible agent, Mike Piranian, advised me that all of the dates had been sold. I asked why we were not called or given the opportunity to participate as white concert promoters had been given. They refused to answer. They spoke to me like I was being a pest. During that conversation the agent, Mike Piranian, made a remark to me that I will never forget. He said in an angry tone, "I am sick of you guys!" I wondered what guys he was referring to and why he would say that. Was it because we were trying to make a living? Was it because we wanted to be treated fairly? Or was it because of the color of our skin?

I later placed a call to Toni Braxton's management. This is when I first met her manager, the infamous Randy Phillips. After I got to know him and he got to know me, he shot straight with me as much as he could. I seriously voiced my concerns about what was happening to the black concert promoters. I informed him that I had been involved with promoting her previous tour. I explained to him that we have decided that the only recourse that we had was to picket and boycott the shows. He quietly listened and when I finished he said he would look into it and contact me later. I received a call a few days later from the responsible agent, Mike Piranian, advising me in a disgusted tone of voice, that he had received a call from Ms. Braxton's manager. He informed me that the dates were priced at $225,000 to $275,000 per show and if we wanted to be involved I needed to send in a fifty percent deposit.

After doing the math, I saw that the shows would have to sell out to make a minimal profit. The risk was too great. I thought this may have been one of the old tricks that they have always used in the past to deter black concert promoter participation, but I wasn't sure. By this time, I wasn't feeling very good about the situation. I asked why we would have to send in a deposit when the shows were already on sale. He had no choice but to agree. They allowed me and the other black concert promoters to participate as a one-third partner in ten shows of the forty date tour. We were also allowed to choose the dates that we wanted to participate in. I didn't feel having involvement in only ten dates was fair, but something was better than nothing. And at the time, we needed something.

From October through December of 1996, I personally attended all ten shows that we were allowed to participate in. I also conducted settlement on our behalf. The look on the face of each white concert promoter as I arrived told me that they resented me being there. That was okay because I felt strongly that we had a right to be there. Some treated me with respect, such as Jules Belkin of Belkin Productions in Ohio and Irv Zuckerman of Contemporary Productions in St. Louis. Others tried to cheat me out of the one-third portion that we were due, like Rick Franks of Cellar Door in Detroit. How they would do this is by pretending that the profits were less than they were. The way this is done is by falsely inflating the show's expenses.

What I learned and observed during the course of these shows sickened me to the highest degree. I was never the same again. The artist payment guarantee per show was not $225,000 to $275,000 as was told to the black concert promoters. It was only $150,000 to $175,000 per show for the white concert promoters. I also learned that none of the white concert promoters had been required to pay a 50% deposit of $137,500 per show, as we were required to do. The deposit for them varied from zero to 10%, ($17,500) of the guarantee. We had been bamboozled and tricked for decades by CAA and The William Morris Agency; I became sick to my stomach knowing what they had done to us for so many years.

From 1997 to 1998, I wrote letter after letter to CAA, The William Morris Agency, and The Howard Rose Agency as president of the Black Promoters Association. I pleaded for a meeting of some sort so that we could discuss the problems we were enduring and had been enduring for the past decades. My letters all went unanswered. I knew then that they had no intentions of working this or anything out with us.

Chapter Three

Tricky Tactics by the Agencies

Tricky Tactics by the Agencies

In 1997, long before the Janet Jackson Velvet Rope Tour was announced I began calling CAA. This was the same agency that oversaw the Kenny G - Toni Braxton Tour. This agency is one of the top and most powerful agencies in the world. I really hated dealing with them for obvious reasons. First of all, I knew they hated dealing with us. Secondly, we had a difficult history when dealing with them. But I had to try to work with this agency because they represented the majority of the top entertainers in the world – black or white.

I spoke to Janet Jackson's agent, Rob Light, on a constant basis expressing my interest in bidding for her upcoming national tour. I was making these early calls trying to circumvent the many excuses that we as black concert promoters have always been given. They would always say to us "you're a little too late", "you should have called earlier", or "the tour is already sold, but next time we will keep you in mind". These are typical excuses always given to black promoters when a tour is being planned for a superstar black artist at CAA or The William Morris Agency. It is true that black promoters are always a little too late, but the reason being is that we are never informed or given notice that a tour is being planned like the white concert promoters are given. It's like when trying to purchase a home you must first know that the house is for sale. These excuses were always used, especially when the artist had the potential to create huge box office sales.

I had known Janet Jackson personally since she was sixteen years old. As I mentioned earlier, in 1979-80 I was chosen by her family to be the national tour promoter for her brothers, The Jacksons. In February of 1998, Rob Light, Janet Jackson's agent responded to my earlier calls. He informed me that planning for the Velvet Rope Tour was about to take place and that he would get back in touch with me in a few days to give me more details. I knew from the sound of his voice that he was planning a trick for me and the other black concert promoters. He sounded rather sarcastic; he didn't sound sincere. I must admit I had no idea what that trick would be. I did know one thing; it would be extremely unusual for him to deal with us fairly. I also didn't expect for him to give us the same equal opportunity that would be given to the white concert promoters. I knew that Rob Light didn't care much for me, but for some strange reason, I liked him. I really believed that his hands were tied and because of the way the concert industry is set up, he could not be fair with us or give us equal opportunity. I never mentioned it to him, but when talking to him I could feel that deep down in his heart he was a decent human being.

Later that week, Rob Light called again and informed me that the minimum guarantee would be $300,000 per show for forty shows. I knew that he thought that this high guarantee would eliminate me, as well as all black concert promoters. What he didn't know however, was that I had prepared for this by contacting some financial lenders earlier and secured whatever financial backing I needed for the 50% deposit. I immediately faxed over to him an offer for $300,000 per show as he had requested. I received no reply. A few days later, I faxed over another letter reiterating my offer and asked for a response. The following week, I received a letter in response to my offer. It advised me that CAA was requiring a 50% deposit of the total guarantee of $12 million. I was prepared for the amount, but then, the real trick came. They also asked for a letter of credit securing the balance of the guarantee. The 50% deposit guarantee and the letter of credit were both due before tickets could go on sale. Rob Light's letter stated that this was the same deal that was being offered to "all" promoters. I felt this was put in place so I could not use any of the ticket proceeds to help secure the deposit.

The 50% deposit was standard for all black concert promoters, but the additional letter of credit was not. Because he had told me that the tour would consist of forty shows, this meant I would have to come up with the entire $12 million, before I was allowed to put tickets on sale. I was prepared for the $6 million, which represented the 50% deposit, but to obtain a letter of credit from a bank or lending institution I would have needed an additional $6 million on deposit in an account at that bank which I didn't have at the time.

Now, here comes the real kicker. In Rob Light's letter that was faxed to me, he gave me until close of business that same day to provide proof of the $12 million. I was sitting in my office when I received this letter by fax. I looked at my watch and I had five hours remaining to raise the $12 million that had been requested. I knew that the purpose for this was to not give me enough time to do so. Unable to secure $12 million in five hours, I was told that I did not meet their demands. The tour was given to a white promotion company in Ohio called Magic Works. I later asked Rob Light if Magic Works paid the $12 million up front as I was requested to do. He assured me that they did. But he was not telling the truth.

Later, I found out that Magic Works was not required to come up with the $12 million at all. They only had to put up a $3 million dollar deposit prior to tickets going on sale and then another $3 million after tickets went on sale. This gave them enough time to sell shows to other promoters such as myself, and raise the money. They were also allowed to pay the remaining 6 million dollars in installments of $150,000 each night of the forty show tour. By being allowed to do this they were able to use the nightly proceeds from each show for payment. As always, we were tricked again by CAA.

The heartbreak was revealed later when I found out that the deal with Magic Works had already been made when Rob Light was going through the motions with me. I ended up participating as a one-third partner in three shows -- New York, Los Angeles, and Washington, DC. I had to purchase them from Magic Works at a cost of $375,000 per show.

I also found out later that Janet Jackson had put a stipulation in her contract with CAA stating that they were to make a meaningful effort to involve black promoters in her tour. This was never told to us at that time. So what CAA did was ask a black concert promoter from Detroit, Billy Sparks, to serve not as a concert promoter, but as a consultant for the entire tour. Billy Spark is a dear friend of mine and has been for many years. He remains one of the best individuals that I have ever met during my years in the entertainment industry. This way CAA was able to deceive Janet into believing that they had black concert promoter involvement for the entire tour as she had requested. This was another one of their old tricks. By doing this, they were able to keep real black concert promoter participation and compensation at a minimum. We had been tricked, once again, by CAA. Billy Sparks later came to me and said "Rowe, I know that I was only involved in the tour because of your actions and your stand for equality". It is only fair that I give the Black Promoters Association a portion of my proceeds, which he did. Billy Sparks is truly one of a kind.

Whenever any black concert promoters have had the opportunity to promote a show or sometimes a tour, CAA and The William Morris Agency have always shown resentment. They begin to look high and low for anything that could cause a problem for us. If there were none to be found, they would always seize the opportunity to create some. They have always hated for our businesses to have success or to show profitability. Profits were only intended for their white concert promoters. I have found over and over again that when an African American artist of star quality decides to tour, these booking agencies always have the uncanny ability to make the playing field unlevel for black concert promoters and the black business community.

No other racial or ethnic group has had such a profound influence on American music as black artists. They created the unique American art forms of gospel, reggae, jazz, blues, rhythm and blues as well as hip-hop. I find it to be very sad that while black musicians have been pioneers in blazing new musical trails, their music has often been copied or stolen by others. These others have gone on to gain greater wealth and prestige than the black originators.

It's a "no holds barred lock-out" when you complain about the way business is conducted in the entertainment industry. All of the individuals and companies in the industry must act in harmony with each other for this system to be effective, and they do. When you're "blackballed" your record company must let you go. The booking agency must dismiss you or not work on your behalf. No television network will accept you. And if you try to make a movie, the studios have to ignore you too. It's all part of a conspiracy in my opinion. With a simple phone call or a discussion at a private meeting, these powers proactively make the immediate decision to "blackball" someone in a very cold and calculated way.

This method of punishment is kept very secretive and confidential by this industry. They would like for everyone to believe that when your services are no longer needed by anyone in the industry, it just happens to be coincidental. If ever asked about it, they all will deny that it even exists. But *believe me*, it does.

When it has been decided that you're an "uppity N-word"; they will begin to take away your livelihood. Those who survive learn to just play the game – others are nothing but sell outs. There are a lot of black entertainers that portray themselves as being loyal to the black community, but when they deal with the powers of the entertainment industry, they are anything but. They will not rattle the cage.

It's the same thing that black people have been complaining about for years. People coming into our neighborhoods to set up their liquor stores, grocery stores, and pawn shops and then they take money from the black community and we never see it again. It's the same thing with the entertainment industry. They financially rape the black communities of America and we never see those dollars again. If we ask for more business to be given to black people, it is referred to as being "uppity." They tell you to keep quiet and do what they say and you will have a great career. If you don't want to do that your career will be halted.

After I became "blackballed", I had to take a different route. I had to start going directly to the artists to plead my case – like I still have to do now. Whenever I called the booking agencies from that point on, they never would allow me to do business with them. They never would sell me anything. By me going directly to the artist, the agencies accuse me of not following protocol, because I have circumvented them. But what they don't admit is that I had no choice because they wouldn't do business with me anyway.

Right now, practically all of the black concert promoters have been shut out of the industry. The industry has been successful in practically eliminating all of us and putting us out of business. There are no new promoters of significance at all; it is virtually impossible for an independent person to gain entry into the concert promotion business. The black concert promoters have practically been eradicated completely from the process. I truly believe that the ring leaders of this eradication are CAA and The William Morris Agency.

I have always spoken out against the collusion, conspiracy, racial discrimination, and treatment of minorities by the entertainment industry. For some, this has been very harmful to their life and livelihood. For one's profession, whether it's an agent, entertainer, or concert promoter, it can be devastating when becoming a victim of the "blackball" conspiracy. Having the only profession you know and love taken away can be financially and personally painful. This has happened to so many of us over the years.

You know, it's kind of hard for me to explain how this whole thing feels. It's just like a doctor who spent many years going to medical school and after he graduates and passes the medical board, he can't get a job. They've taken our profession away from us for no reason other than our race. They have mistreated us and by doing so they have also mistreated our families, employees, and our community as well. It's awful what they have done.

Like I said before, the black concert promoter serves as a financial bridge for that concert dollar to reach the black community and without the black concert promoter that money is never seen in the black community again. The reality is that our concert entertainment dollars are being used to fertilize the exclusive white residential neighborhoods in America like Beverly Hills, the Hamptons and commercial districts like Rodeo Drive. Our black neighborhoods never see those dollars again.

It's from this pain that I am forced to explain the pitfalls of this industry. I have been pretty fortunate and blessed because I have still been able to take care of my family. But I must admit, I just haven't been able to accept what they have done and are still doing to blacks and minorities as a whole.

It's strange how you can reflect on something from your past and see things so clearly, I suppose that old saying is true, "hindsight is twenty-twenty". Looking back on the past two decades, we were the guys who brought entertainment to black America.

Just name any show that entertained the black community and I promise you the majority of the time one of us was involved. What most people don't know was that we had carried these shows around this country under some of the most strenuous contractual agreements that one could imagine, contracts that were designed for us to lose in most cases.

In 1979, before all of this started happening, my career in the concert promotion industry was on the fast track. This had been a very good year for me; my first child was born that year. I named her Robyn. In that year alone I was able to promote over one hundred shows. Not to mention, the other black concert promoters I knew were doing very well also. We helped to advance the careers of many artists that are celebrated all over the world such as Stevie Wonder, Lionel Richie, Michael Jackson, Boyz II Men, and Whitney Houston. Even though those years were good to us, unfortunately since the industry is so fickle for black concert promoters none of us had much to show for our success. We may have a home or a car or two to show for it, but that's it; and to me that's shameful. All of us have families and employees we care for deeply, and by this point we were all struggling to keep our heads above water. In fact, some of us were sinking. These days we are lucky to get any shows. At this point, it is a daily struggle for us to maintain our personal obligations, and to keep our businesses afloat. Little did we know, we were being forced out of business. For all who read this, I want you to understand that all of this transpired because it was planned. It wasn't just the luck of the draw or bad luck; it was a systematic approach to permanently exile black concert promoters from the concert promotion industry, the only profession that we know and love.

One thing I noticed was that white concert promoters that started around the same period we did were flourishing. All of them were doing exceptionally well financially. All had quietly become multi-millionaires. What the industry wanted us to believe is that all black concert promoters were going bankrupt and out of business, and all white concert promoters were experiencing enormous success, just happened to be coincidental. When I realized what was happening, I started to examine the industry very carefully, and one thing was clear to me; the black promoters were not allowed to profit in the industry. I had a mad parade of questions storming through my brain: "What is causing the disparity? Are they treated differently by the powers that control the entertainment industry?" As I will explain later, these are some of the same deceitful tactics that lead to the untimely demise of Michael Jackson the King of Pop.

Chapter Four

The Evil side of the Entertainment Industry

The Evil Side of the Entertainment Industry

In January of 1998, the situation had gotten worse. I was becoming increasingly frustrated with the inability of black promoters to obtain a fair opportunity to compete in the concert promotion business. Shortly thereafter, I had heard from some of my business associates that the African American singing artist, Maxwell, was planning his upcoming tour. I was reluctant to do so, but I contemplated calling his booking agency, which was The William Morris Agency. It was one of the top booking agencies in the world, if not the top booking agency in the world. I went ahead and made the call anyway. I asked to speak to Maxwell's agent. I knew there would be problems ahead. The music department at this agency was now headed by Richard Rosenberg and Peter Grosslight, the executives that once headed The Jackson's previous booking agency. These were the people that gave me so many problems years before. I asked to speak with Maxwell's agent, Jeff Frasco, whom I had known for a number of years. I met Frasco when he first started in the business. He was then an agent at The Norby Walters Agency. A few years later, he became an agent at The William Morris Agency. He had a reputation for being, excuse my expression, a "butthole" when dealing with blacks and minorities. After a few callbacks, I finally got him on the phone. I inquired about the Maxwell tour and the opportunity to bid on his upcoming dates. He confirmed to me that Maxwell was indeed planning to go on tour and as always, he promised to include black promoters.

Within the next forty-eight hours, I submitted firm offers for seven cities on the Maxwell tour. The William Morris Agency had received a lot of complaints in recent times about their treatment of blacks and minority concert promoters. So I felt that this would give them a great opportunity to prove us all wrong and try to dismiss past allegations of discrimination. I was wrong.

About a week or so had gone by when I heard that the Maxwell tour had been distributed to the usual white concert promoters that were members of the so called "good ole boys" network around the country. After that, I immediately contacted Jeff Frasco again and inquired further about the Maxwell tour. He refused to talk to me about it. I knew from past experience what it meant when they refused to talk or pick up our calls. It has always meant that black promoters, as well as the black business community, were being tricked or shut out.

I tried very hard not to be angered by the actions of Jeff Frasco and Cara Lewis, another agent at The William Morris Agency who always had treated black and minority concert promoters in an undignified manner. I always felt that they were only doing what they were instructed to do by their superiors which were Richard Rosenburg and Peter Grosslight.

I immediately scheduled a conference call with all members of the Black Promoters Association to discuss the situation. We decided during that conference call that we would contact a civil rights organization in Atlanta that had been working with us. After speaking with them, we collectively decided to make preparations to picket the Maxwell tour. When The William Morris Agency became aware of our intentions, they hired a former prominent African American basketball player (and a client of The William Morris Agency) by the name of Earvin "Magic" Johnson and inserted him as lead concert promoter of the tour. Although they gave Johnson fifty percent of each date on the tour, I knew this was being done to keep all legitimate black concert promoters out.

I also believed it was being done to deceive the public, specifically the black community, and to give the appearance that a black concert promoter was promoting the tour. In actuality, they kept all of their white concert promoters of the "good ole boys" network in place and involved in their perspective markets. They gave them the remaining fifty percent of each date. It has always been amazing to me the steps that they would take to keep black people and the black business community from prospering.

After thinking about the situation for a few days and contemplating very strongly about what I should do, I decided that perhaps it would be beneficial for me to try and contact Maxwell himself. I thought that this way I could explain to him what they were trying to do to the black concert promoters and black business community. I emphatically felt that he had no knowledge of the treatment that they were trying to perpetrate on the black concert promoters. Later, I called his manager, Randy Hoffman, several times and tried to speak with him. He would never pick up my calls or to my knowledge the calls of other black concert promoters. This manager was a member of the "powers" that controlled the entertainment industry.

After never receiving a return call from Maxwell's agent, Jeff Frasco, or his manager, Randy Hoffman, I decided to spread the word through the Black Promoters Association that I was trying to get in contact with Maxwell himself and needed any assistance that I could get. I later received word from one of my colleagues that Maxwell was staying in Los Angeles at the Sunset Marquis Hotel where I used to stay years ago. I knew the management staff at this hotel very well. I thought that it may be beneficial for me to draft a letter and try to get this letter to him as soon as possible. I wrote the letter explaining the trials and tribulations that the black concert promoters were experiencing in trying to be involved with his tour. I gave very specific details about our frustration and our intentions. I explained that black concert promoters were not being allowed to participate in his upcoming tour. I also explained the trickery tactics that they were trying to use by involving the basketball player, Magic Johnson. I immediately faxed the letter over to the hotel and asked the manager, who had been a long-time friend, to make sure that Maxwell received it. He said he would.

The following day, I received word from a member of the Black Promoters Association that Maxwell had cancelled his entire tour. From that time up until recently, Maxwell had disappeared from the face of the earth -- or from the entertainment industry, I might say. I feared that he had become a victim of the "blackball" conspiracy. I hoped and prayed that he hadn't because if he had, I would surely feel responsible.

Over the years, I've been approached time after time by young, ambitious individuals with a desire to go into the concert promotion business. They would always ask the same question, "How do I get started?" It is so disheartening for me to tell them the truth. The truth being that nowadays it is virtually impossible to gain entry as an independent concert promoter. I hate to admit it, but it is the truth. I consider getting into the concert promotion business as an independent concert promoter to be a long shot these days, a very long shot. It's just extremely hard to do and if you are an African American, it's virtually impossible. You may be able to promote a small show with an artist that does not have much appeal or any significant value. But it is virtually impossible for you to get CAA, The William Morris Agency, or any of the major booking agencies to sell you a major artist with phenomenal ticket selling power and a proven history of doing so. It just won't happen.

It was difficult enough getting in this business when I started over thirty years ago, but with the creation of billion dollar companies, such as Live Nation and AEG, it is virtually impossible to gain entry now. With the insertion of these two companies, the agencies have raised their level of control in the concert promotion industry. I truly believe the booking agencies would like for these two companies to be the only means possible for artists to tour. This would give them a tighter hold and complete control of practically all artists, as well as the concert promotion industry. This assures that the artists have no other outlet for touring other than Live Nation and AEG. This was created by design. I truly feel that this is the exact trap that Michael Jackson was forced into. I will explain later in detail.

Being the masters of control continues to be very lucrative for the booking agencies. If it was in the best economic interest of the booking agencies to have as much competition as possible, as they say it is, why not open the doors to competition or solicit and sell all entertainers to all qualified buyers with no regard to one's race, religion, or national origin? They have never done so and without federal intervention they never will.

In the 1990's, white concert promoters began purchasing their own amphitheaters. This was being accomplished by a number of factors. First, because of the relationships with the agencies, they are able to guarantee that a certain number of shows would play at these venues each year during the summer months. This guarantee could be passed on to the sponsors in lieu of million dollar contracts for the concert promoters. Sponsors such as Miller Brewery, Anheuser Busch, Coca-Cola, and Pepsi, just to name a few, have provided millions of dollars for these promoters in the form of sponsorship deals. Because of this "good ole boys" network, these promoters have been able to guarantee these sponsors that a specific number of concerts, black and white, would play these venues each year.

No single black concert promoter has ever been able to obtain such a lucrative sponsorship deal that would enable him to make such a purchase. Because of the discrimination and conspiracy that has existed within the industry, black concert promoters cannot guarantee the amount of contractual shows needed per year to obtain such lucrative deals. We, as black concert promoters, have always been limited to the promotion of black artists and never received the opportunity to promote white artists. This makes it virtually impossible for me or any other black concert promoter to acquire and maintain amphitheatre ownership.

Before white concert promoters began seeking amphitheater ownership, I attempted to engage in a contractual agreement with the city of Atlanta. In 1984, I submitted a proposal to the city to become the exclusive concert promoter for the city-owned amphitheater at Chastain Park. Around February of that year I met with Mayor Andrew Young at his office to seek his assistance. He was very cordial. I was advised by the mayor that the local white concert promoter, Alex Cooley, had also sought the contract with the city. I knew he was a part of the "good ole boys" network, but I continued with my fight for the city contract. Later that year, the city realized that I could not bring white acts to their amphitheater, which was in an exclusive white neighborhood in Atlanta, while Alex Cooley could bring both black and white artists. Needless to say the contract was awarded to Alex Cooley. Because of my race and the discrimination of the industry, I was denied the right to obtain this contract with the city.

In 1992, a black promoter in Memphis by the name of Fred Jones approached the local white concert promoter there, Bob Kelly, to form a partnership and become the exclusive concert promoters at the local amphitheater owned by the city. When they agreed to do so, they formed a partnership corporation called Island Events. They successfully entered into an exclusive agreement with the city to promote concerts at the city's amphitheater. This was enabled and accomplished because the city preferred that a minority be involved. Fred Jones was personally involved in the promotion of all shows produced at this amphitheater from 1993 to 1997.

Early in 1998, their corporation, Island Events, renegotiated its exclusive contract with the city. A draft of the new agreement was approved by the staff of the Memphis Parks Commission. On March 4th, 1998, the manager of the commission sent a draft of the agreement to the park commission board for its review. On March 27th, the white promoter, Bob Kelly, died. As a result, a new agreement was drafted in which the black promoter Fred Jones was to have an exclusive concert promotion agreement at the amphitheater for two years. A potential third year was contingent upon performance.

On April 17th, 1998 the black concert promoter, Fred Jones, informed Mayor Willie Herenton that the park commission had approved his exclusive agreement for the amphitheater. Three days later, on April 20th, 1998, the board of the Memphis Park Commission formally approved the agreement with Fred Jones. Also on April 20th, Fred Jones made a crucial mistake he faxed letters to CAA, The William Morris Agency, and other top booking agencies in the country. He advised them that his corporation would begin to exclusively book the amphitheater in Memphis. His mistake was that he faxed the letters before the signing of the agreement.

The following day, Barry Leff, Vice President of Beaver Productions from New Orleans, Louisiana, a member of the "good ole boys" network, wrote a letter to the director of the

Memphis Park Commission Board. Barry Leff stated in his letter to the board that he understood that they were considering an exclusive agreement on the future of their amphitheater for that summer. Leff wrote that he wanted to inform them that because of the unfortunate circumstances with Bob Kelly that Beaver Productions had been asked by the top talent agencies in the country to establish an office in Memphis. He was to begin immediately booking all venues in the area. He also stated in his letter that because of his past relationship with Bob Kelly, the deceased concert promoter that he had always stayed out of the Memphis market.

When I saw this letter it totally solidified what I had known all along. To me it provided proof of the conspiracy and collusion between the agencies and white concert promoters. We all believed that we knew where Barry Leff of Beaver Productions received his information. The very next day, the chairman of the Memphis Park Commission wrote a letter to Fred Jones, the black concert promoter. The chairman advised him that the mayor had suddenly determined that it would be unwise to execute a new exclusive agreement with his company. After six years of having this exclusive contract with white concert promoter Bob Kelly involved, Mayor Herenton and the Memphis Park Commission cancelled the Fred Jones' agreement. During the same timeframe, The William Morris Agency had already sold a show featuring the white artist, James Taylor, to Kelly and Jones before Kelly died. It looked like a white artist was finally going to be promoted by a black concert promoter, Fred Jones. Needless to say, The William Morris Agency cancelled the show with Jones and gave it to Beaver Productions, the concert promotion company from New Orleans who wrote the letter.

In the mid- to late-90s, a business conglomerate, SFX, with billions of dollars in assets wanted to break into the business of concert promotion. I believe that they immediately found out that it was virtually impossible and were hit with the reality that they were not allowed to compete with the dominant white concert promoter's monopoly, no matter how much money they had. They had to use the strategy of buying the dominant white concert promoter's companies for hundreds of millions of dollars to gain access to their markets

SFX did not have to purchase black concert promoters because black concert promoters were not given a monopoly on their territories as the white concert promoters were given. SFX is now known as Live Nation.

Unlike most businesses in this country, for example, when Burger King wanted to sell hamburgers, they didn't have to buy McDonald's to compete. They simply opened their own restaurants down the street or next to a McDonald's and competed. This doesn't happen in the concert promotion industry. For the past thirty years, I cannot recall one independent concert promoter of significance that has gained entry in the concert promotion business.

These territorial monopolies were and still are used to maintain harmony among the white promoters and to protect the promoter's relationship with the agency. For example, if an agency sold to the dominant promoter in New York, Ron Delsner, a show in Chicago, the dominant concert promoter in Chicago, JAM Productions, would object. Their relationships with each other and the agency would be adversely affected. If this were to happen in each of the many different markets across the country, the conspiracy would collapse. For the same reason, if any open and competitive bidding were allowed, it would have the same effect.

Like I stated before, black concert promoters were always sold shows in other black concert promoters' territories. This was done so that the harmony that was being experienced by the white promoters could not be had by the black concert promoters. This strategy was used to create a hostile environment among us.

Because of what I believe to be an illegal syndicate, they are able to control the artist, as well as the artist guarantees and ticket prices. This ultimately raised their percentage intake with no opposition from anyone. The white concert promoters operating under these guidelines, in a parallel fashion, have been handsomely rewarded. All have been guaranteed multi-millionaire status, which all have received to the exclusion of all black and outside concert promoters. They are given territorial exclusivity. This arrangement benefits the agencies and concert promoters by giving them total dominance and control of artist guarantees and ticket pricing without opposition. Competition has never been welcomed in this industry.

Controlling the industry and destiny of all involved has been and remains very lucrative for the booking agencies. They are able to control the destiny of all artists, the venues in which they play, and the concert promoters for whom they work, as well as the talent cost and ticket prices.

By this time it was February 1998. I had become exhausted and frustrated from trying to reason with CAA and The William Morris Agency. I had done everything possible to get these agencies to stop their discrimination against us and give us equal opportunity. It was like running into a brick wall. I was so tired I would often find myself praying and asking God to please soften their hearts and allow them to show us compassion. It never happened.

I felt at this point that the only thing left for me to do was try to find a law firm that would be willing to take on my case and file a complaint for me in the federal court system. God knows I really hated to do this, but the booking agencies and white promoters left me no choice. I knew that they were not going to voluntarily relinquish the stronghold that they had on black promoters. It was too profitable. This is the same type of trap that Michael Jackson found himself caught in by the powers of the entertainment industry. They had him tangled in a web that he could not break free of. I will explain this in detail later.

CHAPTER FIVE

THE LEGAL BATTLE BEGINS

The Legal Battle Begins

The first thing I had to do was find a law firm that believed in my case and would be willing to take it on a contingency basis. There was no way I could afford litigation such as this. It would be too costly. I knew it wouldn't be easy to convince someone to do this for me because the music business can be very complex. If someone has not dealt with this industry before it can be very hard for them to understand. I truly believe this is one of the main reasons they have been able to get away with their wrong doings for so long.

One afternoon, I was talking on the telephone with a songwriter friend by the name of Wayne Garfield who lived in New York City. I was explaining my situation as well as my frustration with the industry. I also mentioned to him that I was looking for a law firm that I could talk to about taking my case. He suggested that I speak to his lawyer an attorney by the name of Bob Donnelly. Donnelly was not a litigator, but Garfield thought I should speak to him anyway for some advice. He thought that Donnelly would be able to advise me of some law firms that may be interested in taking on my case.

I immediately made the call to Donnelly the same day. I must admit I was pleasantly surprised. First of all, I was able to get him on the phone with my first phone call. The next thing I liked about him was he seemed like a very honest attorney, and believe me honest attorneys are very hard to come by these days. He was also an entertainment attorney, so he had some knowledge of my situation. This made it very easy for me to explain to him the problems we as black concert promoters were having. I really liked Donnelly. He stated to me that he understood very well the problems that we were having, and he said that he would make some calls to some law firms that he had worked with and would call me in a few days. I gave him all of my telephone numbers and thanked him for his time. I really felt good about Donnelly. Not only did he sound honest, he was a perfect gentleman.

For the next few days, I waited patiently for his call. About a week later, I received a call from him. Donnelly said he had met with a law firm by the name of Gold, Farrell & Marks and that they might be interested in taking my case. He also stated that it was a very good and reputable law firm in New York City. He wanted to arrange a meeting for all of us to talk. I told him that I would be available whenever they were ready. He called me back later that afternoon to advise me that the meeting had been set for the following Monday afternoon.

I flew out of Atlanta bright and early on that Monday morning in February. I arrived in New York about 12:45 p.m. that afternoon. I caught a cab and went straight to the law firm of Gold, Farrell & Marks. The meeting was set for 2:00 p.m. that same day. I entered the building, got on the elevator, and went up to the law firm's floor. When I arrived at the floor, Bob Donnelly, as well as two other attorneys, Martin Gold and Christine Lepera, were all waiting on me. Martin Gold was the senior partner.

We went to Martin Gold's office to begin our meeting. He first ordered refreshments. He then asked me to explain the situation. I began explaining to them the discrimination we had faced when trying to conduct business with the two top booking agencies in the music industry, CAA and The William Morris Agency. I went on to explain how all of the black concert promoters were being mistreated and shut out of the business by these agencies.

I gave further examples of the discriminatory treatment we had received. I went on to further explain at length the disparity in treatment between blacks and whites by these companies. Gold was very understanding and showed a lot of compassion. I really liked these attorneys and this law firm. The meeting lasted for about two hours. When I finished explaining, Gold said that they wanted to do some investigation into the matter and would contact me in a few days.

About two weeks had passed when I received a call from the New York law firm. I was at home in Atlanta at the time. Martin Gold first advised me that Christine Lepera was also in the room with him and that they would like to put me on the speakerphone. He asked if that was okay. I replied, "Yes." He stated to me that they had concluded their investigation and found that the allegations and complaints that I had made seemed to be valid. They thought that I had a very good case not only against the top two booking agencies, but against all of the booking agencies and white promoters in the concert business.

He stated that all of the agencies operated in a parallel fashion and they were all breaking the law. He also stated that they were all in violation of our civil rights. He then said that they would like for me to return to New York as soon as possible so that we could prepare an agreement and begin forming the complaint. I said to them that I would arrange my schedule so that I could return as soon as possible. I told them that I would give them a call when I was ready to come. This was around the end of February.

Two months passed. It was now mid-April and I had not called them back to schedule the meeting. I think I was still looking for a better solution than this one. Please remember at the time I was closing in on the age of fifty and this business was the only profession I had ever known. I guess I was still hoping that the booking agencies would change their ways.

A week later I received a message at my office from Christine Lepera at Gold, Farrell & Marks. Her message stated that they were waiting to hear from me so that they could set up our meeting and to please call. Still feeling a little hesitant I did not call.

Over the next couple of months, our treatment from CAA and The William Morris Agency got worse. They wouldn't sell us anything and wouldn't talk to us about it. They weren't picking up our calls at all. They continued to be very blatant and arrogant with their discrimination. You could tell that they didn't care what we thought or what we did. They conducted business like it was their God-given right to discriminate against black people. It was now August 1998; I felt that the only thing left for me to do was to call the New York law firm of Gold, Farrell & Marks to set up an appointment so we could begin preparing the complaint. I called and set the appointment for the following week.

When I called they said that they would begin preparing the agreement. They also stated that they would forward over a draft of the agreement the following day for my review so that when I arrived in New York it would be ready for signing. We also discussed other black concert promoters that I felt should be included as plaintiffs in the lawsuit. They asked me to make that decision and contact them. I want you to remember that up to this point I had not mentioned this to anyone. No one in the music industry, black or white, knew what my intentions were.

I really had to think about this one. I knew this would be a critical decision and I had to personally think about each black concert promoter individually before I approached them. I had to try and decide who would have the heart and the courage to engage in a battle such as this one. I knew each and every one of these guys, and I knew that some didn't have the heart and some didn't have the courage. So I had to be very careful with whom I confronted to engage in this endeavor.

First I called my closest colleague at the time, concert promoter Alan Hayman in Boston. We had been business partners and promoted shows around the country together for about twenty years. We had seen some good times together and we had seen some bad times together, but I was still a little hesitant about telling him. I knew I had to because I couldn't do this without at least allowing him the opportunity to be involved. I explained to him what I was doing and what my plans were. I also told him that I had already contacted a law firm in New York and they were willing to take our case on a contingency basis. He abruptly stopped me and said, "Rowe, let me do this with you." I said to him, "You know I will -- you are my boy." He would become Plaintiff Number Two.

The next call I made was to a concert promoter out of Jackson, Mississippi, Lee King. This concert promoter had not been active for a few years because of the discrimination that he had endured. He was one of the concert promoters we had recently invited to join the Black Promoters Association. I chose this concert promoter for a number of reasons. First of all, he had been in the business a long time. I knew that he had the heart and the courage to engage in this type of fight with the industry. This concert promoter also had great integrity and impeccable character. I knew that I could surely depend on him. I loved this guy. He would become Plaintiff Number Three.

I then made a call to a concert promoter in New York City, Jesse Boseman. I had worked pretty closely with this concert promoter when the opportunity had permitted. I had spoken to him on a constant basis for years about the discrimination and racism within the concert industry. I knew that Boseman would have the heart and courage to take on this fight. But what I didn't know was if I could fully trust him. I felt that if a good enough offer was ever presented to him, he would not hesitate to betray us. I must admit that this concert promoter still had certain qualities that I felt we needed. I made the decision to include him and hoped for the best. He would become Plaintiff Number Four.

The next promoter I contacted was a concert promoter out of Memphis, Fred Jones. This was the concert promoter I previously discussed that lived in Memphis. He had been around a few years longer than I had. He was very well known throughout the music industry and was somewhat respected as a very good local promoter in Memphis. I didn't always agree with his thinking and decision making, but he had some qualities that we surely needed on board with us. First, like I said previously, he was well known. Secondly, he had done pretty well in other business ventures that gave him financial stability. I felt that he had the heart and the courage, but I knew that at times he could be difficult to deal with. Nonetheless, I thought it would be best to include him. I called and explained to him about the attorneys and what our plans were. I then extended to him the opportunity to be involved. He said very quickly, "Count me in." He would become Plaintiff Number Five.

I felt that all was set now and we were ready to move forward, but then a few days later, I received a call from another concert promoter who lived in Charlotte, North Carolina. He was also a member of the BPA. His name was Bernard Bailey. He said that he had heard about what we were planning and asked to be included. I kind of liked this guy, but he had been involved in some illegal fraudulent activity pertaining to the concert promotion industry in previous years. I didn't want this to hinder us in any way. So I told him that I would think about it and call him later. I'd had some legal problems of my own unrelated to the concert business in past years, so who was I to judge? I thought we should give this guy a chance. After all, he'd been around for some twenty-five years at this point and he really needed this opportunity. I called him back and told him that he was in. He was delighted. He would become Plaintiff Number Six.

I then contacted the attorneys in New York and told them of the choices that I had made. They immediately set up a conference call so that we all could talk. During this call the lawyers explained everything to us and answered our questions. They told us to gather up all evidence in the form of contracts, letters, and documents that we had in our possession, especially if they showed any sign of discrimination. They told us that they would be setting up a phone interview with each of us to discuss our previous history with these agencies and concert promoters.

About the first week of September 1998, I returned to New York to meet with the attorneys. When I arrived at their office they were again waiting on me. I could tell from Gold's and Lepera's demeanor that they had something to talk to me about. They were moving swiftly. After we were seated, they explained that we were not going to only sue the top two booking agencies, CAA and The William Morris Agency we were going to sue all of the agencies, because we believed that all of them were guilty. Gold said to me that we also had to sue the concert promoters, because we also believed they were all guilty as well. They also said to me, we are not only going to sue for discrimination, but also for violation of the anti-trust laws. Then both partners looked me straight in the eye as Gold said to me that they felt that I had a very strong case. They also believed what was being conducted here was a conspiracy.

I knew what they were saying about the other booking agencies and concert promoters was true, but my main focus had always been on the top two agencies, CAA and The William Morris Agency. I knew they were right in what they were saying because none of the agencies had ever sold us any white artists or given us equal opportunity. For a great length of time I had always seen collusion between the agencies and the white concert promoters, so this was not shocking to me. I knew that they had the correct assessment of what had been happening and I saw that they had really done a thorough investigation.

After discussing the situation with Alan Haymon, Plaintiff Number Two, we knew we had to make one exception. This exception would be a booking agency by the name of International Creative Management (ICM). This agency was about the third largest in the country, if not the second. It was true that this agency had never given us equal opportunity or sold us their white artists, but this agency was the reason that our businesses had not completely closed.

ICM had a white agent for many years by the name of Phil Casey. He was responsible for booking the majority of the black artists at this agency. Over the years, he was the responsible agent for such artists as Puff Daddy, Boyz II Men, New Edition, and many, many more. Unlike CAA and The William Morris Agency, when their black artists became superstars they always took them away from black concert promoters and gave them to the white concert promoters. This agent never did that. Casey would always allow us to continue booking their black artists after they reached star status. He was the reason that we were able to feed our families and keep our businesses alive. What a heck of a guy Phil Casey was.

I later relayed this information to the attorneys. They didn't like it, but they had no choice but to accept it. For the next couple of months, the attorneys did a great job compiling evidence and preparing the complaint. By now I was speaking to the attorneys on a daily basis trying to get the complaint completed.

In October 1998, we had another Black Promoters Association meeting at the Hyatt Hotel in downtown Atlanta. At this meeting we discussed with everyone what our plans were and entertained any questions that they had. We also talked about our future as concert promoters and what was mandatory for us to do if we were to remain active.

The week prior to this meeting, a member of the Black Promoters Association who lived in Washington, D.C., Bill Washington, decided to quit the organization after hearing of our intentions. This promoter was still enjoying what I would consider to be somewhat of a cordial relationship with The William Morris Agency. Not that he was receiving equal opportunity by any means, but they considered him to be a good ole fellow who rattled no cages. The William Morris Agency would allow him to promote a show every now and then and I believe that because of our lawsuit and being associated with the Black Promoters Association, he strongly felt that the little livelihood he had left might be jeopardized. I understood completely. This is my opinion.

After the Black Promoters Association (BPA) meeting, a promoter from Los Angeles, Larry Bailey, also resigned. I was not surprised about this promoter resigning. I had always been told by other BPA members that this promoter would never be involved in a confrontation with the top agencies -- namely CAA. I was told that he did not have the heart or the courage to engage in this type of battle.

After the meeting, Alan Haymon, Plaintiff Number Two, asked to see me in private. We went over to the hotel where he was staying. He began explaining to me that for personal reasons he had to withdraw as a plaintiff in the lawsuit. He did not know it, but I had already heard that he was in negotiations with the billion dollar conglomerate, SFX, to sell them a percentage of his company. I was not upset with him at all. This was a great opportunity for him and his company. I considered this to be a deal of a lifetime. With the business changing the way it was, this was something that he could not pass up.

I had previously told him that sooner or later he was going to be approached with a deal. I didn't know by whom at the time but I knew it would happen. Up to this point, SFX had no black concert promoter involvement at all. With all the light that we were shedding on racism and discrimination in the industry and with the lawsuit coming, I knew that they would have to involve a black concert promoter sooner or later. Haymon was the best choice.

On November 19th, 1998, we filed the complaint in federal court in the Southern District of New York. The war was about to begin. The filing of this lawsuit made the front page of all entertainment magazines and took very high priority in all newspapers, radio, and other publications.

Shortly thereafter, I arranged a meeting with Dr. Joseph Lowery, a well-known and respected civil rights leader. He was also a close ally of the late Dr. Martin Luther King, Jr. He already knew of our circumstances because I had met with him on previous occasions. I explained to him what we were doing and asked for his assistance in the future. I knew that he had a very heavy schedule with speaking engagements and public appearances, but he still volunteered to help us whenever his schedule would permit. He later became the father I never had.

Whenever I was confronted with an important decision, I would always consult with Dr. Lowery first.

Over the next few weeks, I was flooded with requests for interviews and telephone calls from people applauding what we had done. I must admit one thing. At this point I was harboring something in my mind that I could not forget or shake. In the late 70's, I had the privilege of having another famous civil rights leader assist me in confronting the same problem I was having now, the problem of discrimination. His name was Hosea Williams, and he was also a close associate of Dr. Martin Luther King, Jr. In 1979, he had flown with me to Los Angeles to meet with the executives of The Jacksons' booking agency. After a very heated meeting, we returned to the Sunset Marquis Hotel for dinner. During our dinner he said something to me that was now constantly on my mind. As we were discussing this industry he said," Rowe, listen to me, and listen well. Never expect a Jewish person to defeat another Jewish person for you, especially when the stakes are high. It just will not happen." Considering the fact that we had sued these booking agencies for $700 million, I considered the stakes to be high, very high.

Now, I must admit this situation presented a huge problem for me mentally. It constantly stayed on my mind because the stakes in this case were not only high, they were huge. Despite growing up in the South and often being mistreated because of my race, I can honestly say that I have never been prejudiced or anti-Semitic in my life. But it remained hard for me to forget what he had told me mainly because our leading law firm in New York was Jewish and the people we were fighting were also Jewish.

God knows, I didn't want to jump to conclusions, but I began putting all correspondence in writing with this law firm. I made a request to see all documents pertaining to our case, incoming and outgoing. I was really hoping that I could trust this law firm and that they would prove my friend wrong. I also thought about our case being litigated in New York, a city that had a lot of Jewish control and connections. I was hoping this law firm would not betray me. I tried to put all of this aside and out of my mind because I really liked this law firm.

There was one thing I felt good about, that is our case was in the federal court system and not the state court system. I thought we could trust the federal courts better than the state courts. Shortly after, a federal judge was assigned to our case. His name was the Honorable Robert P. Patterson. He was a very seasoned judge. He had been on the bench for over ten years. I immediately did some investigation into his background. I found out that he was a Republican and I also found out that he had been appointed by President Ronald Reagan in 1988. His being a Republican made me a little nervous because I had always heard that Republicans were not too strict when it comes to civil rights. But to be honest with you, I really had no proof of this.

A month or so later, the defendants filed for dismissal of our complaint. They cited that our claims were baseless and there was no discrimination in the concert industry whatsoever. They also stated that no anti-trust laws had been broken. This was to be expected. About a month and a half later, the court heard oral arguments on the defendants' motions to dismiss. They argued vigorously that the allegations that we were making were all untrue and unfounded. They stated over and over again that there wasn't any discrimination in the concert promotion industry and no conspiracy had existed. They also stated that some of us were not even concert promoters. They said that black concert promoters were able to promote any and all artists, black or white, if they chose to do so. They also stated that everything in our complaint was false.

Martin Gold argued for us and his argument was horrible. He did not mention one time that black concert promoters were not allowed to promote white artists. This was the foundation of our case, but he never once mentioned it. I truly thought he had lost his mind. I didn't know what he was doing or what he was thinking. It was awful. I knew we would not defeat this motion. When I returned to Atlanta, having not been able to accept the oral argument of Martin Gold I immediately called him bright and early the following Monday morning. I said to him, "I cannot believe what you have done." I also said "You argued our discrimination case and not one time did you mention the fact that black concert promoters are not allowed to contract with white artists." I told him I thought he had lost his mind. He had nothing to say.

On May 29th, 1999, we received Judge Patterson's opinion and order. He dismissed our complaint in its entirety. Our claims against all defendants were denied. The good thing was that our complaint was dismissed without prejudice. Which means this gave us the opportunity to re-file our complaint. Although this was disheartening, I was still thankful that the judge gave us another opportunity. What was very strange to me was in Judge Patterson's opinion and order he explained exactly what we needed to do in order to get the amended complaint to prevail. It was like giving us a road map. I was very thankful for that.

On August 9th, 1999, we filed our complaint again. In legal terms this is referred to as the "amended complaint." A short time after, the defendants filed their motion to dismiss again. By this time, I had hired a law firm from California to assist us, the law firm of Ivie, McNeil and Wyatt. It was a law firm I had found in Los Angeles through a close friend. This was a black law firm and I had heard that they were a pretty good law firm.

The attorney that I was dealing with at this firm was Rickey Ivie, one of the partners in the firm. I decided to hire Rickey Ivie, thinking that this would give me a close companion not only to work with us on the case, but someone who would look out for us and keep us aware of everything that was going on.

I felt I needed someone of this caliber because I was still somewhat watchful of our New York law firm. Over the next few months I spent a lot of time speaking to Rickey Ivie and watching his demeanor. I liked him as a person, but as an attorney he did not meet my expectations. I was disappointed with him. He seemed to have a great deal of fear about vigorously fighting these defendants. I also thought he became too close with John Rosenberg, attorney for the defendant, The Howard Rose Agency. He never seemed to understand who his client was and where his loyalty should lie.

Shortly thereafter the courts heard oral arguments again. The defendants put up the same argument as they did before, stating that all of our allegations were false. Martin Gold argued for us again, but this time, he did a remarkable job. He stated everything about how we were treated in the industry and why it was done. He also thoroughly explained to the court that black concert promoters had never been allowed to contract with white artists. I was very pleased with his performance.

This judge really impressed me a lot. I could tell that he was a seasoned judge. There were a lot of attorneys in the courtroom about forty I would say. We had sued twenty-eight concert promoters and seven booking agencies. At the end of the hearing, Judge Patterson asked that all lawyers please take their attorney hats off for a second. He stated that this was a very ugly case and he did not like this kind of case in his courtroom. He also said to the defendants' attorneys that it would collectively cost their clients in the neighborhood of possibly

$100 million to defend this type of lawsuit. He asked them not to do this injustice to their clients. He further stated that he believed that they could sit down with the plaintiffs' attorneys and work something out that would be cheaper than it would be to try and defend this type of case. The defendants' attorneys did not mumble a word. I knew they were not going to try and work anything out with us, especially CAA and The William Morris Agency. They were too defiant when dealing with black concert promoters. To work this out with us also meant that they had to stop the collusion and discrimination and they surely were not going to do that.

We waited patiently again for the judge's decision. Our lawyers had told us that we should hear something from the court around the first of the year. January 2000 had passed and it was now February. We had not heard a word from the court. We waited and waited. I was a nervous wreck by this time. I was spending a lot of time praying and asking God to be with us.

March, April, and May had come and gone. By now it was mid-June and we still hadn't heard a word. I began to worry. My mind began to turn. What kind of tricks are they trying to play on us now? I could barely sleep at night.

It was now Friday, June 30th, around 4:00 p.m. in the afternoon. I had left the office early and I was at home lying across my bed trying to get some rest. I had not slept well the night before. My phone rang and I decided to let the answering service answer it so I could continue my nap. My phone immediately rang again and again. Still, I did not answer as I was trying very hard to get some sleep. My phone rang yet again and I still refused to answer it. As I laid there, I thought about my wife and kids who were not at home and I said to myself, "Something may be wrong with them." I immediately called my answering service to retrieve my messages. They said to me, "You must call your attorneys in New York as soon as possible. They said it was very urgent!" I knew we had finally heard from the court.

Before I made that call I immediately got on my knees and began to pray. I prayed to God that he had allowed this judge to rule fairly and that he wouldn't allow him to mistreat us as we had been mistreated by the defendants. I also thanked him for everything he had done for me up to this point and asked that he please continue guiding me.

I then got up, picked up the telephone, and called my attorneys in New York. When I called, they were all in Martin Gold's office together. When they picked up the phone, I could hear the joyful spirit in the sound of their voices. They asked, "Leonard, how are you doing?" I began to weep and said, "I'm doing fine." I knew we had won. They began telling me that they had received the judge's opinion and order, and that we had prevailed on all counts against the defendants. I was so thankful; I could only find the strength to utter the words, "Thank you, thank you, thank you." I immediately called all of the other plaintiffs and informed them of the good news and of the judge's decision. I then drove to see my wife Regina at her job to tell her face–to–face.

Shortly after, I began looking for another law firm to join our case. I felt that for me to find the type of attorney I needed, I would have to look in the South. I remembered something that Dr. Joseph Lowery had told me. He said during the Civil Rights Movement, they could not find people from the North or the West who were willing to fight discrimination as vigorously as those in the South. He said that it was no accident that almost all of the civil rights fighters came from the South.

As our case progressed, it was now the year 2001. I received a call from the president of the Agency for the Performing Arts

(APA). This was one of the booking agency defendants in our case. The president's name was Jim Gossnell. I had known Jim for a few years but had not spoken to him for quite some time; maybe fifteen years or so. He said to me that this didn't make any sense to him and asked if I would fly to LA and meet with him. I said I would. We scheduled a meeting for that following Friday. I flew to Los Angeles and met with Jim Gossnell. He was a very nice guy. The meeting went extremely well. It lasted about two hours. At the meeting we decided to settle our differences for a minimal amount and I agreed to release APA from the case. This was our first settlement.

I called and informed my attorneys of the decision. They were okay with it. I knew this would alienate CAA and The William Morris Agency as they knew they were the guiltiest ones in the litigation. They also knew it would take a great deal of money for us to settle with them. Not as much as they had taken from us, but a great deal nonetheless. They did not want any of the defendants to settle with us. Like I had always heard, "misery loves company" and they wanted as much company as possible. CAA and The William Morris Agency tried their very best to hide their agony, but I knew all along they were truly miserable. The strangest thing about this entire situation is that it did not have to be. All I ever wanted from CAA and The William Morris Agency was to sit down with us and try to find common ground that would allow black concert promoters the opportunity to work and make a living. They always refused my offer to do so.

By this time we had started picketing and protesting at the office of CAA in Los Angeles. We picketed everyday from 10 a.m. to 6 p.m., Monday through Friday. We had from twenty to thirty picketers on a daily basis. These were people that did not possess much in life in the way of monetary value, but they were very dedicated to us and our cause. I will forever love them all!

My mind stayed focused on finding another attorney; I didn't know what to do. I was worried. I knew I needed more help in our case. One day after finishing our protest march in front of CAA, I returned to my hotel in Hollywood. Like most days I was exhausted. I took a shower, cut the television on, and laid across the bed. The program *60 Minutes II* was coming on. One of the featured stories was about this black attorney from Stuart, Florida, by the name of Willie Gary. I immediately focused in and listened. After hearing him talk and explain how he vigorously fights for his clients, I felt this was the attorney I needed. He also said that companies that he litigated against would always spend a lot of money litigating to defend their discriminatory practices. He went on to say that he would always fight vigorously for his client's civil rights. I said to myself, "This is the attorney that I need!"

The task would be how I would get in touch with this attorney. I had no idea how to accomplish that. The following week after I returned to Atlanta, I thought about Dr. Joseph Lowery. He seemed to know everybody. I immediately picked up the telephone and called him. I asked if I was disturbing him. He said, "No." I went on to ask him if he knew this attorney in Florida by the name of Willie Gary. He said, "Yes, I know him very well." I asked would he be kind enough to see if he could contact him for me and set up a meeting for me to speak with him. He said he would be glad to, if he could locate him and that he would try to contact him immediately.

About fifteen minutes had passed and I received a call back from Dr. Lowery. He said he had spoken to Gary who was in Atlanta at the courthouse in the middle of a trial. He told Dr. Lowery to tell me to come down to the courthouse and we could talk while the jury was deliberating in the case that he was involved in. It was pouring down raining that day, but I jumped in my car and rushed down I-75 to the courthouse downtown. He was waiting for me when I arrived. We went into a small office where we could talk. I explained to him about our case and brought him up to date. I asked him would he please come on board with us. He said he had already heard about this case and that he would love to come aboard. I was ecstatic!

I called all of the plaintiffs and informed them of the news. I then called the New York attorneys and told them about my decision to bring Willie Gary on board. At first they were a little apprehensive about it, but later they thought it would be a great idea.

Shortly after, we began the discovery phase of the case. This included the taking of depositions and the inspection of documents by both sides. We began immediately forming our team to do document inspection of the defendants' files. The defendants were all in different parts of the country so we assembled approximately four different teams. These teams included attorneys as well as plaintiffs, Lee King, and me. As we were doing the document inspections we simultaneously began doing the depositions. The plaintiffs were to give depositions first. I had asked our attorneys to schedule Lee King from Jackson, Mississippi first, Fred Jones from Memphis, Tennessee second, Jesse Boseman from New York third, Bernard Bailey from Charlotte, North Carolina fourth, and I would be last.

I wanted Lee King to go first because I knew they would not be able to trick or trap him with their questions. I also knew that he knew the business very well. I felt that he would be a great choice to go first. I had a lot of confidence in Lee King. Next was Fred Jones. I didn't worry too much about Fred either. I thought he might have been capable of making a small blunder here or there, but I didn't think he would make a major error. I must admit I was a little worried about Jesse Boseman for various reasons. I knew that the defendants' attorneys would be tricky and try and trap him with their questions. I didn't know whether he could handle that or not. I was just hoping that he would be able to hold up. Bernard Bailey was next. I knew that Bernard had a pretty good knowledge of the business so that didn't worry me much. What did bother me is that I knew that Bernard had some business-related legal problems in his past. I knew they wouldn't be asking him too much about the nature of our case, which was discrimination, but would try to destroy his credibility and character.

I could tell all along that the defending attorneys knew that their clients were guilty. However, it was their job to try to get them out of this trouble, and they were in a lot of it. They had some of the best law firms in the nation such as Loeb & Loeb, Weil Gotshal, and Winston and Strong representing them. This made no difference to me at all because I knew one thing, they were guilty and we had them red-handed.

All of the plaintiffs had done pretty well at their depositions except for Bernard Bailey. Like I thought, they worked on his past legal problems and tried to destroy his character and his credibility. They didn't ask him too many questions about whether he had received equal opportunity or not. Nor did they ask many questions about his ability to contract with white artists. They knew the answer to those questions. They mainly asked him about his past legal problems.

My deposition was to be next, which would be the last one. It was to be a four-day affair Monday, August 13th, to Thursday, August 16th, 2001. I packed four suits and flew to New York where my deposition was scheduled to be taken. I arrived the

10

day before. I was not worried at all about them trying to trick me or trying to get me to say something wrong. I knew all I had to do was tell the truth and I surely knew that the truth was not on their side.

I arrived in New York and checked into my favorite hotel, the New York Helmsley on 42nd Street. It was late on the afternoon of August 12th, 2001. The place where my deposition was to be held was four blocks away. I got up the next morning and went to meet my attorneys at their office. After a short meeting, we proceeded to the deposition. I was accompanied by Maria Sperando of the Willie Gary firm and Richard Primoff of Gold, Farrell and Marks. There were so many attorneys there you could have sold popcorn and peanuts and made a hefty profit. I could tell that they really wanted to get to me. I was considered the villain in this case, the one who started all of this. They really wanted to destroy me, but I was not worried.

I was first questioned by John Rosenberg, The Howard Rose Agency's attorney. After about an hour of questioning, I could tell that he was becoming frustrated. They then began asking me, about some things that had happened some twenty years ago in my past when I had some returned checks and other unrelated matters. I knew at that point they were reaching for straws. He was not able to accomplish his goal of destroying my credibility. Then, like now, they use the strategy of trying to divert ones' attention from the main issue at hand. Instead they talk about things that are totally unrelated. This is the same deceitful tactic that is being used today when those that are responsible for the death of Michael Jackson are confronted with questions about the pop stars' untimely demise. The problem that they were dealing with was that their clients were guilty, and they knew it. I had pretty good knowledge of the entertainment business, so I had no fear of him creating a problem for me. As my questioning continued with all of the attorneys, I could see the disappointment on their faces. They were not accomplishing what they wanted to accomplish with me. I could clearly see the frustration.

After my deposition, we were all feeling pretty good. As we were packing up and preparing to leave, I asked one of my attorneys, Maria Sperando, if I could speak to her in private. She said, "Yes." I quietly asked her to keep a watchful eye on everything and everyone that was involved in our case; not only the defendants, but our own attorneys as well. I explained that these defendants, especially CAA and The William Morris Agency, would do anything to get out of this case. I explained that we had the type of case where if anyone was in the position to help the defendants they could acquire enormous wealth. I then stated to her that the type of wealth I was talking about would be very hard for anyone to turn down. They could name their price. I felt that CAA and The William Morris Agency would pay anyone that they had to pay, except us, if they were in a position to help them eliminate this problem. She seemed as if she got insulted and immediately walked away.

It was now the middle of September 2001 when I received a call from Maria Sperando. She informed me that she had spoken to the New York law firm concerning Bernard Bailey. She said that they all felt that because of his poor performance at his deposition he could hinder us in fighting our case. She stated that Bailey had too many problems in his background for a jury to show us any type of mercy. She said it would be in the best interest of everyone if Bernard Bailey resigned from the case as a plaintiff. She then asked what I thought. I asked her to give me some time to think about it and I would call her later.

I didn't want to just throw Bernard out. I knew over the years he had been discriminated against like the rest of us, but I did not want him to hinder our chance of prevailing. Shortly after, I had to make the decision to ask Bernard Bailey to resign as a plaintiff. He did not want to, but he knew it would be in the best interest of everyone for him to do so. He finally agreed to resign. Now there were only four plaintiffs left.

CHAPTER SIX

THE LITIGATION

The Litigation

By this time, the deposition of the defendants was about to begin. I was really looking forward to this. At the same time, we were still doing document inspection of the defendants' files. I had also requested a computer disc of all the defendants' documents, so that I could personally review them at home and at my office. Although I had firsthand knowledge of the discrimination and collusion that existed, I was still not prepared for what we found in the files of CAA, The William Morris Agency, and The Howard Rose Agency. The things they said about African Americans were horrible. They became unbearable for some of us to view.

Howard Rose of The Howard Rose Agency was about to begin his deposition next. I had been up late that night viewing his files on my computer. It had to be about 1:30 a.m. in the morning. I was looking at his contracts and saw the disparity in treatment between black and white concert promoters. This was not surprising, but as I came across the Lionel Richie file I saw something that was not only surprising, but shocking. What I found was a handwritten note, written by Howard Rose himself, pertaining to the Lionel Richie tour that stated **"no Blacks"**. The reason I was up so late looking at Rose's files was because his deposition was scheduled for the following day in New York. It was to be conducted by Maria Sperando of the Willie Gary Law Firm.

Without getting any sleep, I rushed to the airport and flew to New York bright and early that morning. I had my findings from Rose's files in my possession at that time. When I arrived in New York and presented what I had found to my attorneys, they could not believe what they were seeing. Sperando presented that document that said **"no Blacks"** to Howard Rose immediately at the start of his deposition. She asked him, "Whose handwriting was that"? He replied, "It looks like mine." She asked him to please read the document into the record; he did. She then asked him what he meant by the statement **"no Blacks"**. He paused for a few minutes and then said, "I can't recall." Howard Rose knew he was finished at that point. The rest of his deposition did not seem to matter.

A month later, Rose's attorney asked to settle. This is when I became totally disturbed with my own attorney, Rickey Ivie. He thought we should accept an offer from Rose that I felt was totally insulting. I knew that he had become friends with John Rosenburg, Rose's attorney; well, I guess I should say he thought they were friends. This was not surprising to me, and from that point on, I was finished with Ivie as my attorney. He stayed on the case, but I had no more use for him. We ended up settling with The Howard Rose Agency for twice the amount that Ivie thought I should have accepted.

By now the courts were hearing our motion on the defendants' e-mail. This was new territory for the courts. We were asking them for permission to review the e-mails of mainly CAA and The William Morris Agency. The agencies did not want to comply with this request. They came up with every excuse in the world for why they should not have to submit to this. First they stated it would be too costly. They said it would cost hundreds of thousands of dollars for them to extract their e-mails. They also said it would be an invasion of privacy to their artists and would give black concert promoters the advantage in booking them. What a joke. They would not allow us to book Celine Dion or Madonna even "if we knew the brand of underclothes they wore". Prior to our request, our attorneys researched the cost related to the e-mail extractions and it wasn't near the cost CAA and The William Morris

Agency said it would be. After going back and forth with this issue for months, the court finally granted our request. The judge's ruling required us to provide the company that would be extracting the emails and to also cover the cost for extracting them. I was very happy about the judge's ruling, but there was still one problem. We did not have the money to pay for the e-mail search. I felt confident that we needed this evidence, so I knew that we had to get the money from somewhere.

By this time, Clear Channel had purchased SFX, the conglomerate that owned all of the white concert promoters. Clear Channel, being a publicly traded company, did not like the type of publicity that came along with this type of lawsuit.

It was now November 2001, and we were in LA taking the deposition of one of Clear Channel's employees, Bruce Knapp. I had heard from my conversation with a black agent who at the time was with ICM, that Knapp visited their agency about a year before. While Knapp was in the agent's office with some other employees of Clear Channel, he overheard the conversation where Knapp referred to him in a derogative racial manner. Talking to someone on the phone, he heard Knapp say, "I am in the **spook's** office." This agent became very angry and asked Knapp and his fellow Clear Channel counterparts to leave his office. Knapp was asked about this at his deposition and admitted that it did happen.

Willie Gary, of our new law firm, had planned a press conference in New York to publicize our lawsuit and his coming on as one of our attorneys. I thought this was a great idea. The press conference was to be held the following week in front of one of the Clear Channel offices. I received a call from Willie Gary a few days before the press conference was scheduled. He stated that we were going to cancel the press conference. I asked him why. He said that he had received a call from Ray Heslin, one of the attorneys from our New York law firm. He said that Heslin had asked him to cancel it until we got more information. By now, I had become very suspicious of this New York law firm. I felt that Heslin was only trying to protect Clear Channel.

I had learned that Heslin had been a long-time friend of Clear Channel's attorney. This was too close for comfort for me. What I decided to do was schedule a press conference in New York myself. I first contacted Dr. Joseph Lowery, and asked him if he would assist me in organizing the conference. He said he would not only assist me, he would commit to being the lead spokesman as well. I then called my dear friend, the Rev. Al Sharpton. He also made a commitment to participate. I also contacted a PR firm that had been seeking business from us for quite some time. I asked them would they come aboard and handle the PR for the press conference. They accepted. We began immediately sending out invitations and inviting all of the media outlets to be present.

A few days later we received word that Clear Channel wanted to settle. The settlement negotiations were scheduled to take place at Harvard University Law School in Cambridge, Massachusetts. I was only told about the settlement negotiations two days before it was scheduled to take place. I was now becoming very suspicious of Martin Gold, and his New York Law Firm. The mediator would be Charles Ogletree, a professor at Harvard University Law School. I immediately called our other attorney, Willie Gary and told him about the settlement conference. He knew nothing about it. The New York law firm had not informed him of it either. I knew immediately that they were trying to play tricks with us. I believe the reason for not informing Gary was because he was not wanted there, mainly by Martin Gold and Ray Heslin. I believe they felt they could get a better settlement for our defendant Clear Channel if Willie Gary was not present. But they had one problem; they could not have the settlement conference without informing me.

When I informed Gary, he told me he had another settlement conference scheduled for that same day. He said he would move it to another time period so that he could attend ours. The next evening Gary flew to Atlanta on his private plane to pick me up. He was accompanied by Maria Sperando and his son, Saku Gary, also an attorney at his firm. We arrived in Boston around 10:00 p.m. that night. We checked into a hotel very close to Harvard University.

The conference was scheduled to begin at 9:00 a.m. that following morning. We all arrived on time for the conference and the negotiations began. The negotiations lasted all day. After going back and forth, we finally stopped around 7:00 p.m. that night with no settlement in place. But we were not far apart, we were close. To be frank with you I was ready to take their offer, but Gary wasn't. He had more experience at this than I could ever have, so I was not going to intervene. I really thought we should have taken their offer. The e-mails and the expenses we needed to cover were constantly on my mind. I knew that without this settlement, we would not be able to cover our expenses and get the e-mails. I was sure the e-mails would expose everything.

When we got in the car to leave, Gary saw that I was worried. He said to me, "Rowe, don't worry, they will call tomorrow with a better offer." We left that night and I returned home to Atlanta. The very next evening I received a call from Willie Gary. He said to me he had received a call from Clear Channel, and they were willing to raise their offer. He then asked me what I wanted to do. I replied very strongly, take the offer, and we did. This settlement would give us the money we needed to keep fighting. Most of all this gave us the financial ability to retrieve the e-mails from CAA and The William Morris Agency.

By now our New York law firm of Gold, Farrell & Marks had merged with another law firm by the name of RubinBaum. Our lead attorney, Martin Gold, had quietly begun to remove himself from our case. I was becoming more and more suspicious of him and his law firm. At the time I did not know why he was doing this. He had told me in the beginning this was his pet case. He was also the one I had entrusted to handle this litigation. At that time, he assured me that he would always be the attorney that would be working with us. As we continued our document inspection of the defendants' files and were finding crucial evidence, Gold showed no interest in what we were finding. He had backed away completely from our case. He now had assigned his associate, Ray Heslin, to oversee everything. This guy, in my opinion, was the perfect example of a flunky. I had no respect for him as an attorney whatsoever. Heslin may have been the overseer of our case, but I knew that Martin Gold was orchestrating everything from behind the scenes.

I was in New York one day at the office of RubinBaum doing document inspection of the defendants' files. I was standing outside of Ray Heslin's office waiting to see him when I overheard him telling someone about a meeting they had with our defendants the day before. This was very alarming because I had not been told about this meeting. By now, Martin Gold was avoiding me as much as possible. I could tell that he did not want to face me. I was beginning to feel that something unethical was happening with this law firm. I thought again about Hosea Williams and what he had told me. I began to worry and wonder if we were being betrayed.

The Litigation

By now the e-mail company that Marty Gold hired had retrieved the e-mails from CAA and The William Morris Agency. I was told that it would take approximately six weeks for us to receive the results of their findings. The way this was explained to me was that we had to provide certain keywords to the company that was retrieving the e-mails for us. When those words were found in any of the e-mails, the documents would be revealed. The company also said they would give an accurate account of how many times each word was used. We presented words to them that were considered racial slurs such as "nigger," "spook," "blackie," "monkey," and a list of others were given as well. I waited patiently for the results of the e-mail search to return. I was confident that the e-mails of CAA and The William Morris Agency would tell all about their wrongdoings and solidify our allegations of discrimination and collusion. I also felt this would put our case to rest. At the same time I also knew that if the e-mails returned with damaging information for the defendants it would put Marty Gold in a position to name his price. It would be like hitting the lottery for him. That price could be, as it should be, for his clients, or it could be for himself. I truly, truly believe he chose the latter.

It was now July 2002; the day had finally come for the results of our e-mail search to arrive. I woke up bright and early that morning. I waited patiently for Marty Gold and the rest of the attorneys at the New York law firm to arrive. I began calling them about 10:00 a.m. that morning. I first asked to speak to Richard Primoff, the attorney that was handling our case on a day to day basis. I could not get him on the phone. I then began calling Martin Gold. I was not able to get him either. I then asked to speak to Ray Heslin. God knows I hated to talk to this guy, but I was very anxious to know the results of the e-mail search. He was not available either. At this point, I was really wondering what was going on.

About two hours had passed and I had not received a return phone call from anyone. I thought this was very strange. They knew I was waiting on the results, so I couldn't help but wonder why they wouldn't return my calls. I decided to wait until after lunch before I called again. Around 2:00 p.m., I began calling everyone again. I was still unsuccessful in reaching anyone. It was now around 6:00 p.m. that evening and I knew it was time for them to leave for the day. I picked up the phone and tried calling again. This time I was successful in reaching Primoff. I asked him what was going on and explained that I had been trying to reach them all day. He made no excuses; he just said that they had been busy. I had talked to Primoff on a daily basis for a few years now and had gotten to know him somewhat well. I can honestly say that he did not sound truthful at all, and he also sounded kind of nervous. I began asking him about the e-mail results and asked if they had arrived.

He answered, "Yes, they have."

I asked, "What did we find?"

He replied, "Not much of anything we could use."

I said, "What did you say?"

He repeated himself again, "Not much of anything we could use." I found this not only to be disappointing, but unbelievable as well. I knew from the sound of his voice he was not telling me the truth. It was now becoming obvious to me that something was surely happening with this law firm. I called the other plaintiffs and told them what was told to me by Primoff. None of them could believe it. We had spent a lot of money retrieving these e-mails and now I believed that a cover-up was happening with our own law firm.

The following week I had to return to New York to speak to Ray Heslin concerning the stipulations of our settlement with Clear Channel. I was sitting in his office in front of his desk talking to him when he received a phone call. He said, "Excuse me for a second," and turned his back to me so that he could talk in private. I happened to look on his desk and saw a stack of papers. At the top of the papers it said, <u>Rowe Entertainment vs. The William Morris Agency E-mail Search</u>. It displayed the number of hits for the racial slurs we had submitted. The first word displayed was **"nigger"**. It was at the top of the list. It showed that the word **"nigger"** had been found **two hundred and thirty-two times (232) in the e-mails of CAA and The William Morris Agency.** I knew now for a fact that I had been betrayed by Martin Gold and his law firm.

When Heslin finished his call I politely asked him, "What is this?" referring to the papers on his desk. He quickly turned them over and said, "You were not supposed to see that." I asked the question, "Why I am not supposed to see it when it is pertaining to my case?" He did not answer. I immediately called The Willie Gary firm and told them what I had seen. They were as shocked and surprised as I was. This information had been hidden from them as well as from us. They immediately called the New York law firm and inquired about the list. Later the list was sent to the Willie Gary law firm. However, they never sent the actual documents that contained the word **"nigger"** or other racial slurs. They only sent the list showing the number of hits that were extracted. Martin Gold never spoke to me about these documents, nor did he ever show them to me. I truly believe he used these documents to cut an undercover deal with the defendants for himself and possible others at his law firm. This is what I truly believe. I must say that I feel totally positive that we were betrayed by Martin Gold and his firm.

We later began doing depositions of CAA and The William Morris Agency executives. These depositions were mainly handled by members of the Martin Gold firm. At the deposition of Rob Light, the head of CAA's music department, plaintiff

Lee King and I were present. The questioning was being done by Carl Aaron of RubinBaum, Martin Gold's law firm. During a fifteen minute break, while in the men's room, Lee King overheard one of CAA's attorney's telling another attorney of CAA that Aaron was not going to ask any hard questions. King returned and told me and Aaron what he had heard. Naturally, we wondered why the attorney would say that. When we asked Aaron, he had a smirk grin on his face and didn't say anything.

Later, I was confronted with another problem with this law firm. Without my knowledge or the knowledge of any of the plaintiffs, Ray Heslin was attempting to file a new complaint. He called me after he got the new complaint prepared. The new complaint would drop our anti-trust claim against the defendants. I asked him what he was doing. He said he was trying to streamline the complaint. I told him our complaint did not need streamlining and asked what he meant by streamlining. He said he wanted to drop the anti-trust claims against the defendants. I told him we were not going to do that. I said if the anti-trust claims were going to be dropped, they would be dropped by the court. I knew by now that this law firm was not only a crooked law firm, but they were also violating the law. It was totally unethical what this law firm was doing to us. By this time Martin Gold had disappeared completely. I had not seen nor talked to him in months.

As our case progressed, the defendants finally deposed Phil Casey, the agent from ICM that had always treated black promoters fairly. He had always allowed black promoters to promote the black artists at his agency. I was present at his deposition. It was held in Los Angeles at the office of one of the defendant's law firms. They became angry with Phil Casey because he refused to lie for them. He would only tell the truth. They wanted him to say that the plaintiffs were not capable of promoting concerts, which was totally not true. Casey refused to say that. They wanted him to speak negatively about me and all of the other plaintiffs, but he wouldn't. He just simply told the truth, and like I said before, the truth was not on their side. I knew they were going to be angry at Casey because he did what he was suppose to do, tell the truth under oath.

After Phil Casey's deposition, I told a close friend who's in the music industry that I was expecting Phil Casey to lose his job at ICM. He said, "no way, Phil has been there over twenty years." I told him that makes no difference to these people. He said, "Phil is about to retire," and I said again, "that makes no difference." About six months later, Phil was released from ICM. I told my friend that those who run this industry are very crafty. They are extremely good at waiting and putting some time between what they consider a betrayal and your "blackballing"; in hopes that you will not be able to relate them to each other. Phil Casey may not be aware of it, but I truly believe if he had lied and spoken negatively about me and the other plaintiffs, he would still be at ICM today. But, I am afraid that he too became a victim of the "blackball conspiracy".

It was now August 2002. We were still picketing at the office of CAA when I suddenly received a phone call from Dan Weiner, the president of Monterey Peninsula Agency, a defendant in our case. It was also right after Michael's protest in New York against Sony Records and Tommy Mottola, which occurred in July, where Michael was also complaining of discrimination. Dan Weiner asked if it would be possible for us to sit down and talk. I told him that at the present time, I was in LA conducting a protest march at CAA. He asked would it be okay if he came to LA for us to meet. I said yes, that would be okay. We arranged a meeting for the following day. He said he would call me when he arrived at his hotel. I received a call from him around 2:00 p.m. the following afternoon. The hotel was not far from CAA where we were picketing. I asked him to give me an hour and I would be over. When I arrived, I called him on his cell phone and told him I was in the lobby. Shortly after, he came down and we proceeded to the dining area to talk.

He began by saying to me the same thing other defendants had also said. He stated he did not understand why Monterey Peninsula was included in this lawsuit. He went on to explain that the guilty parties were CAA and The William Morris Agency, not Monterey Peninsula. When he finished, I began to explain to him that what he said was partially true. I did believe that CAA and The William Morris Agency were the guiltiest parties, but Monterey Peninsula was guilty as well. I continued by asking the question, have you ever done any business with a black concert promoter? He paused for a minute, and said that the artists he represented were mainly white. He also went on to say that he would do business with anyone whether they were black or white, as long as they were reputable promoters. I asked another question, have you ever allowed a black concert promoter to promote any of your white artists? He never gave me one example of that occurring.

I began to explain that I did not for one minute believe that Monterey Peninsula was as guilty as CAA or The William Morris Agency. I believed that Monterey Peninsula was guilty of institutionalized racism. This industry has always operated under the discriminatory policy that black people are not allowed to promote white artists. I told him that I believe Monterey Peninsula was guilty of following this pattern of discrimination. I went on to say to him that in this country of ours, you have the right to choose your business, but you do not have the right to choose the color of people you do business with. And when you begin to do that, you are engaging in what is called discrimination. I must say this guy, Dan Weiner, was a gentleman. Unlike the executives at CAA and The William Morris Agency, he was very pleasant and respectful. I liked him a lot. But I told him I could not release him from the litigation without compensation.

About a week later, he made me an offer to settle the lawsuit with his company, Monterey Peninsula. I refused his offer at that time. I didn't think that his offer was good enough for us to accept. Weiner's deposition was soon approaching. I began thinking about the problems we were experiencing with the New York law firm of RubinBaum. I became paranoid thinking that Martin Gold and his law firm may sabotage our case with Monterey Peninsula as I suspected they were doing with CAA and The William Morris Agency. I quickly called Gary and instructed him to take the offer that had been presented by Weiner. Monterey Peninsula was immediately released from the case.

Shortly after, I received a call from Randy Phillips, Toni Braxton's manager. He asked me to do him a favor and speak to his friend, David Zedeck, of Renaissance Entertainment, another booking agent defendant in the case. He said David was a pretty good guy and he would appreciate it if I would speak to him. This was before Randy Phillips, had any involvement with Michael Jackson. Due to the mutual respect we had for each other at the time, I told him I would be glad to speak with David Zedeck. I asked him to give David Zedeck my number and to tell him to call me. A few hours later, I received the call from Zedeck. He began as all the other defendants had by saying that Renaissance should not be in this lawsuit, that Renaissance was not guilty of anything and that I should allow them to be released. I began to explain to him, as I had done with others that Renaissance had never allowed a black concert promoter to contract with any of their white artists. I also explained that I believed that Renaissance, like Monterey Peninsula was guilty of institutionalized racism. I knew Renaissance had not been in existence very long, only about three to four years at the most, but they represented some of the most highly successful artists at this time.

Their roster included artists such as Britney Spears, N'SYNC, and The Backstreet Boys. I explained to him that black concert promoters had called his agency on numerous occasions trying to contract with these artists, but his agency never granted any of them the opportunity. I asked him why. He could not give me a definitive answer. At the conclusion of our conversation, because of Randy Phillips, I made him a very modest offer to settle our differences and to release him from the case. He refused my offer and I never heard from him again.

I think I knew what the problem was with Zedeck. It wasn't my offer, because my offer was the lowest offered to any defendant. I think he didn't want to alienate CAA, with whom he had a close relationship. I felt he would rather stay in the lawsuit and continue paying his attorney fees which would truly exceed my offer, rather than to settle and alienate CAA. His agency Renaissance later merged with CAA.

By now, we had settled with most of the defendants. A settlement had been reached with Clear Channel, which included all of the promoters except two. The final two were Beaver Productions of New Orleans and Jam Productions of Chicago. There were only three agencies remaining. They were CAA, The William Morris Agency, and Renaissance. We all knew that CAA and The William Agency were the guiltiest of all of the defendants, and I knew they would do anything in the world rather than settle with us. I also knew one other thing. They would pay or do whatever was needed to prevent them from facing a jury and stopping the integration of the concert Promotion Industry. My only problem was that my attorney, Martin Gold, and the judge in our case, The Honorable Robert P. Patterson, also knew the same.

It was now September 2002. I had arrived back in Los Angeles late Sunday afternoon to continue our protest march and picketing of CAA. Monday evening around 4:00 p.m. while picketing, a gentleman walked by me and gave me a note. The note asked me to call a certain young lady that worked at CAA. The note said that she really needed to speak to me and to please keep this confidential. I immediately thought this was a trick being orchestrated by CAA. But for some reason after about thirty minutes, I went to my car and made the call. The young lady answered the phone. She told me who she was and asked if she could meet with me. She said she had some information that she thought would be beneficial for what we were doing.

Still feeling a little skeptical, I arranged to meet her that afternoon. We set the meeting for 7:30 p.m. in my hotel lobby. She arrived fifteen minutes early. She said she did not want to go all the way home after she finished work only to return to Hollywood for our meeting. We decided to go to my room where we could not be seen. We sat at the table in my suite and she began to explain why she wanted to meet with me. She also said, "Don't be alarmed, I'm Jewish." As she continued to speak, I knew this was not a trick. She began telling me of her employment with CAA and that she had been working there for a number of years. She continued to speak of the discrimination she had seen while working at CAA. She also said that the discrimination at CAA extended further than that of race. She explained that they also discriminated against women. She stated that she had been treated pretty well during her employment, but others had not been so fortunate. She went on to explain that black employees were never given equal opportunity at CAA. She also told me about a situation where a hanging noose had been given to a black employee in the mail room. She also provided me with contact information to reach that employee.

She continued by telling me of another CAA employee by the name of Quenton Embree. I could tell that she had a lot of respect for Embree. She explained how he always spoke out about discrimination at the company. I asked her if he was an African American, and she replied "yes". She said that he would occasionally have confrontations with the president of the company, Richard Lovett. She also informed me he had been employed with CAA for approximately ten years, and he was not afraid to speak out against their policies.

She went on to tell me that she was in a position at CAA that would allow her to pull some letters and documents that would be beneficial to our case. She said she would fax them to me if I would give her my fax number, which I did. She then asked me to please get in contact with Embree. She said that he would be glad to speak with me and that he was a very stand-up guy. She gave me his contact numbers at home and at CAA and asked me to give him a call. Shortly after, I walked her to the elevator and she left.

The following week when I returned to Atlanta, as she had promised, she faxed me one letter and three documents that were helpful in presenting our case. I still speak to this young lady occasionally. What a very nice lady she is. Currently, she is still employed at CAA.

The following day I contacted Embree by phone. I called him at home, so that there would be no fear of anyone listening to our conversation. This guy was unbelievable. Very seldom do you meet someone who works in this industry that is not afraid to speak out against it. Embree was not only willing to speak out, but he volunteered to assist us in any way he could.

The following day while we were picketing at CAA, Embree came out to meet me. I could tell from our first meeting that he was, as she stated, a stand-up guy. He asked if we needed water or anything, and I replied no, we had all we needed, but I thanked him anyway. From that day on, we continued to talk on a regular basis.

It was now mid-October 2002. I was at home in Atlanta when I received a call from Don Fox. He was the principal owner of Beaver Productions, a promoter defendant in our case. Beaver Productions was the company that sent the letter to the Memphis Parks Commission stating that they had been asked by the top talent agencies in the country to establish an office in Memphis. The letter also stated that they were told by the booking agencies to immediately begin booking all venues in the area. I was very surprised to receive his call. I had been told by a close associate who was a promoter, that Fox had a reputation for being somewhat arrogant when dealing with black people. I must admit, he spoke cordially, but I could tell he really hated making this call. He sounded as if he resented having to talk to me. The conversation was short. He asked me about releasing him from the lawsuit. I told him I would be glad to, but he must first make compensation for his company's wrongdoings. He said he would have to think about it and that he would get back in touch with me later. I never heard from him again. I was later told by one of his attorneys that Mr. Fox had said if he had to pay anyone he'd rather pay his attorneys and I guess that's what he decided to do.

As our case progressed with motion hearing after motion hearing and the deposition of the remaining defendants and their employees, I was anxiously awaiting the opportunity to bring our case before a jury. I knew that CAA and The William Morris Agency would spend millions of dollars fighting us. But with the evidence mounting against them, and it was, I was sure they would spend even more not to face a jury. This is what worried me.

I personally attended each motion hearing. At each hearing, Judge Patterson would plead with each defendant to settle the case. He would say to them that with the evidence he saw, it would be hard for them to overcome it at trial. He also stated to the defendants that by settling, they may have to change their ways. He then went on to say, "That's life". I could always tell that this judge was not fooled by the defendants. He knew all along that they were guilty.

For the next few months, I pleaded with Richard Primoff of our New York law firm to depose Embree, the employee at CAA. I had told him all about Embree and some of the things that Embree had told me. I also told him that Embree had asked to be deposed and that he would have a lot to share about the acts of discrimination at CAA. I knew all along why he was hesitant to depose Embree. He knew that his testimony would probably hurt CAA. By this time, I was well aware that Martin Gold and his law firm which was now Sonnenschein Nath & Rosenthal did not want this to happen. I had found that sometimes attorneys have the tendency to forget that they are the employee and not the employer. I immediately told him that if Embree is not deposed immediately, I would get Gary of our law firm in Florida to do it. The following day, he sent out a deposition notice for Embree. The notice requested for the deposition to be held in two weeks. We received word back from CAA's attorney that Embree would not be available on that day. What they didn't know however, is that I was speaking with Embree on a regular basis. He told me that he had not been notified by CAA or the attorneys concerning this deposition, and he was available on that date. Soon thereafter, Primoff was contacted by the CAA attorneys, and they asked that the deposition be postponed for three weeks. We had no choice but to agree.

During the next three weeks, the executives at CAA began to be extremely nice to Embree. They even asked him if he wanted to be an agent. They said they would put him in training very soon. Embree felt this to be very hilarious. He knew they were only trying to keep him from telling what he knew about CAA at his deposition, but it did not work.

I personally flew to LA to attend Embree's deposition. Embree immediately began talking about the discrimination at CAA and he never stopped. He spoke about every discriminatory act he could think of during his employment at CAA. He also spoke of the negative treatment towards African Americans and the racist statements he had heard during his employment there. It was a horrible deposition for CAA.

The year 2003, was slowly approaching and the discovery phase of our case was coming to a close. We had taken the depositions of black concert promoters, Alan Haymon, Bill Washington, and Billy Sparks. We had also taken depositions of Richard Rosenburg and Cara Lewis of The William Morris Agency, Rob Light and Carol Kinzel of CAA, and many others. We had enough testimonial and material evidence on the remaining defendants to the point that I thought they would have to be insane to go any further. Boy, did we have damaging evidence and we had a lot of it. But you have to keep in mind that by CAA and The William Morris Agency settling the case, this would open the industry to free competition and destroy the conspiracy that they had in place. It would also tear down the walls of segregation and the industry would finally become integrated. This is something I knew they did not want.

The judge had stated numerous times that he did not believe in resolving a case at summary judgment. He said he had found it is best to let a case such as this one be decided by a jury. That way, there would be no regrets later. I knew it would be impossible for the defendants to win a summary judgment motion. At first, I did not think they would even try it, but I had to remember that this was CAA and The William Morris Agency that we were dealing with. They would do anything rather than give in to us, a group of black concert promoters.

Summary judgment was slowly approaching when the judge ordered a mediation to see if we could settle the case. The mediation was to be held in New York at the federal courthouse. It was to take place around February of 2003.

Everyone met in New York on a Monday morning. All of our attorneys were present. They included Bob Donnelly, Ray Heslin and members of his law firm, Rickey Ivie from our California law firm, and Willie Gary and Maria Sperando from Gary's law firm. I was hoping we could come to a resolution by having this mediation. At the same time, I couldn't help but think about how defiant CAA and The William Morris Agency were towards us. The defendants' attorneys were there when we arrived and they looked as arrogant as always. The mediation was to be conducted by a magistrate judge by the name of James C. Francis. I was hoping that Judge Patterson would be overseeing the mediation and not this judge. Every time this judge was assigned to oversee any of our motion hearings, he was not favorable towards us. I had always felt favoritism for the defendants coming from this judge. Up to this point, after five years of litigating this case, I had never felt that about Judge Patterson. Even when he ruled against us on certain motions, I felt it to be fair.

The mediation began with each side conferencing separately with Judge Francis. The defendants went first and as I expected, made no offer to settle. Our attorneys went next and asked for an offer from the defendants. The judge told Willie Gary, that there was no offer made. I knew that their minds were set not to give us anything. I was okay with their arrogance and their defiance. I felt sure that a jury would give us compensation for how we had been mistreated. We left that day as I had expected with no settlement.

A month or so later, Martin Gold and his law firm asked to be dismissed from the case. They sent me a letter asking me not to object to their dismissal. They also said that if I did object, they would tell the court that they did not believe in our case any longer and that they now did not think that our allegations were valid. If you can remember, Martin Gold and his law firm were the ones that first not only told me how valid our case was, but also told me that we had to sue all of the booking agencies and all of the white concert promoters, which I agreed to do.

But after seeing all of the evidence that directly showed discrimination by the defendants, which included the word "nigger" two hundred and thirty-two times in CAA and The William Morris agencies e-mails which I truly believe he tried to conceal, now he no longer believed in our case. Given all of the evidence showing disparity in treatment by the contracts, the statements we found in one defendant's files that stated **"no Blacks"** and a handwritten note by Carol Kinzel found in CAA files pertaining to the Janet Jackson tour, that said "do not divulge guarantee re: black Promoters," and hundreds more pieces of evidence that showed a direct indication of discrimination, Marty Gold and his law firm decided to just walk away. As attorneys often say, it just doesn't pass the smell test. By this time I had found out that this attorney, Martin Gold, was awful.

When an attorney betrays his clients the way I believe Martin Gold betrayed us, I truly feel that they should be disbarred and never allowed to practice law ever again. After six years of litigation, working on a contingency basis, obtaining all of the evidence we obtained, and twenty-seven out of thirty-two defendants having already settled, Martin Gold decided to quit at this late stage in the case and *just walk away*. By this time we've had success with settlements from the majority of the defendants. Everyone could not help but wonder why he would do this. I felt sure I knew very well why. He had committed the biggest betrayal that any attorney could commit, the betrayal of his own client.

Shortly after, Martin Gold and his law firm filed a motion with the court to be dismissed. I did not object to their dismissal because I did not want Gold to say what he had threatened to say although I knew it was totally untrue.

I had known Martin Gold for about six years now. He and his law firm had put a lot of time and hard work into this case. Being this close to the end, and with all of the evidence that had been uncovered against the remaining defendants, he had to be very well compensated by someone to just walk away. This is my belief.

CHAPTER SEVEN

BETRAYAL OF JUSTICE

Betrayal of Justice

It was now February 2003, and not to my surprise, the defendants filed for summary judgment. For the past year or so the defendants had been saying that they were confident they would get out of the case at summary judgment. So what I started to do a year prior to this was study the laws on summary judgment. What I learned was that it was very difficult for the moving party to prevail at the summary judgment level. I also found that there could be nothing in the record in the form of evidence for a defendant to prevail at this level. I *mean nothing* in the form of testimony or material evidence.

The law plainly states that there must not be a *scintilla of evidence* for a defendant to be granted summary judgment. The law also states this is especially true in discrimination cases because evidence is so often buried in testimony. The party who files for summary judgment has the burden of showing that no genuine issues of material fact exist. I knew it would be impossible for the defendants to show that, so I was very confident that we would defeat their summary judgment motion.

There was so much evidence against the defendants, especially CAA and The William Morris Agency, that I could not help but wonder why they would even attempt this motion. Like I stated before, I knew they were defiant but this was taking it to the extreme.

Although I felt positive that we had been betrayed by Martin Gold and his law firm, Sonnenschein Nath & Rosenthal, I still felt that there was too much evidence against the defendants for the judge to grant their motion for summary judgment. The record was filled with facts demonstrating violations of federal laws. The booking agency defendants denied everything and gave explanations to cover up their violations of our civil rights. They tried to complicate what was actually simple to understand. CAA, The William Morris Agency, and other booking agency defendants had denied contractual opportunity to black concert promoters by using their unique position in representing artists. The evidence that we also uncovered showed that when the booking agencies and dominant white concert promoters worked together, black concert promoters could not get a contract.

Despite their denial, the evidence showed that the booking agencies exercised outright control in awarding contracts for tours that black concert promoters were denied the opportunity of getting. The evidence also showed that the booking agencies were in a unique position to conceal, interrupt, and shut down communication that was essential to black concert promoters obtaining contracts. We had put forth evidence showing the court that the booking agencies were in effect the gate keepers for all access to participate in the concert promotion industry.

We had thirty days to file our opposition to their motion for summary judgment. By Marty Gold and his law firm quitting on us at this crucial stage, the Willie Gary Law Firm was left to answer this motion alone. I was asked by Maria Sperando of the Willie Gary Law Firm to come down to Florida and assist them on compiling the evidence and preparing the opposition to the motion. I immediately packed up and flew down to Florida. I made preparations to stay for the entire thirty days. I asked my friend and fellow plaintiff, Lee King, to come down and assist me in compiling the evidence. He said he would be glad to.

It was now the middle of March 2003. I caught a plane out of Atlanta early that Monday morning bound for West Palm

Beach, Florida. I arrived approximately one hour and fifteen minutes later. I rented a car and drove to Stuart, Florida, the home of The Willie Gary Law Firm, which was about forty-five minutes away. I arrived at the law firm around 11 a.m. that morning. I was then taken directly to Sperando's office. She first thanked me for coming and said that she needed me to compile the evidence and present it to her and the other attorneys. She said that we would only be allowed to view the evidence that was labeled confidential and we were not to view the evidence that was labeled highly confidential.

She then took me to the conference room where I was to work. There were approximately one hundred and seventy-five boxes of evidence that was taken from the files of the defendants. I decided to wait until the next day when King was due to arrive before I started. I then left and went back to the hotel to get some rest.

The next morning I woke up bright and early ready to go to work. I arrived at the law firm around 9:00 a.m. and got started. The evidence I began to uncover showing discrimination was insurmountable. Around noon that day, Lee King arrived. The first thing we did was to compile contracts showing zero to 10% deposit requirements for white concert promoters and 50% deposits always being required for black concert promoters. We pulled approximately two thousand contracts showing this disparity. We also pulled hundreds of contracts showing where white concert promoters were given the opportunity to promote black artists, but found none showing where a black concert promoter was given the opportunity to promote a white artist. We also found evidence in CAA files showing collusion between them and the white promoters and found a handwritten memo naming white promoters and showing their territories. At the top of the memo it plainly stated, "territories". We further found in CAA files a handwritten note which showed a direct indication of discrimination. It was pertaining to the Janet Jackson "Velvet Rope" tour. It was written by CAA agent, Carol Kinzel. The note stated, **"do not divulge guarantee re: black promoters."** There were many, many other pieces of evidence that indicated discrimination towards black concert promoters, too numerous to mention here.

In the files of The William Morris Agency, we found much of the same, such as contracts showing the deposit disparity of zero to ten percent deposit for white promoters and fifty percent deposit for black promoters. Another piece of evidence we discovered was advance notice letters sent by CAA and The William Morris Agency only to white promoters. The letters gave the white promoters notice as to the artist and timing for which tours would take place. These letters were pertaining to both white and high profile black artists. No such advance notice letters were ever sent to black concert promoters. When black promoters called to inquire about which artists were touring, CAA and The William Morris Agency would only tell us about the less successful black artists. They would never volunteer any information or give us the opportunity to promote white artists.

During discovery, there were only two artists that gave depositions. They were Bill Cosby and Marlon Jackson of The Jacksons. The booking agency defendants had previously stated that they did not make the decision pertaining to which promoters an artist should use. They said the decision was almost always made by the artist. During Cosby's deposition, he stated that over his career that spans more than forty years, he had worked with a lot of promoters. He estimated that number to be approximately three thousand, but stated that he had only personally selected perhaps ten of the three thousand over his entire career. He stated that The William Morris Agency had selected ninety percent of the promoters he had worked for.

We also learned at Marlon Jackson's deposition, that in his thirty years in the music business while touring with his brothers, The Jacksons and The Jackson Five, the agency almost always selected their concert promoters. This disputed the notion by the defendants that the artists choose the concert promoter.

We continued to uncover evidence upon evidence showing collusion and conspiracy between the agencies and white promoters. The evidence proved that the playing field was not level. It also showed why blacks and minorities could not compete in the concert promotion industry.

As the days progressed, we compiled approximately ten boxes of evidence that was to be presented to the court to oppose their motion for summary judgment. We truly had uncovered more evidence of discrimination and collusion than this, but as I understood it from my attorneys, we did not need all of our evidence for the summary judgment motion. We only needed enough to defeat the motion.

It took the judge almost two years to issue his opinion on the summary judgment motion. On January 5th, 2005, the judge returned his ruling. What he had done was totally unbelievable, as he had dismissed the case against all remaining defendants including The William Morris Agency and CAA. With all of the evidence we presented to the court showing discrimination and violation of the anti-trust laws, Judge Patterson decided for some strange reason to deny us our day in court. This was very painful to all of us. Over the years, I had come to know and respect Judge Patterson. What would make him violate his oath and the law is puzzling to me. What is even more puzzling is four months before he issued his ruling, the word was circulating within the music industry that we had lost our case. At that time I paid it no attention because I knew that a ruling had not been issued, but I know deep in my heart what transpired. It was the same corruption and collusion in which the powers of this industry are used to engaging.

I believed that what I had always feared had come home to roost. I knew all along that our case was a very fragile one. I knew it could fall apart at any given time. We were dealing with a group of companies, mainly CAA and The William Morris Agency, that would do anything or pay any amount to anyone that could eliminate this problem and get them out of this trouble, except us, the plaintiffs. Yes, I do believe the fact that we were African Americans had a lot to do with it. I knew that the evidence that was retrieved from the e-mail search put Martin Gold and his law firm, which was Sonnenschein Nath & Rosenthal, in a unique position to name their price with the defendants. The defendants could not allow the documents that contained the word "nigger" (two hundred and thirty-two times) that were retrieved from the e-mails of CAA and William Morris to be made public.

This would have forever cast a dark shadow on these two agencies and would have also revealed the discrimination and the racism that exists at these companies. I truly believe that Martin Gold and his law firm committed the ultimate sin to their clients, the sin of betrayal.

Like I stated before, Judge Robert Patterson was a person I had grown to respect during the years of this litigation. I can honestly say that I had agreed with practically all of his motion rulings that had taken place over the past five plus years, even when he ruled against us. I could always understand his reasoning behind his ruling. I had come to have enormous respect for this judge. I started to believe that Almighty God had chosen this judge for us, and for some strange reason I still do. I deeply feel that we were betrayed by this judge, the Honorable Robert P. Patterson. He swore under oath to protect and defend the constitution and laws of the United States of America. When I last checked, the law made no exceptions to this requirement. He clearly did not obey the law. I truly believe that the massive amount of money that was at stake here, as well as the illegal way of doing business in the concert promotion industry, played a significant role in his decision. I also believe that all of this and whatever else was needed caused this judge to turn a blind eye and a deaf ear to the evidence, and take away our basic right as citizens to have a jury hear our case. I also believe that our race also played a significant role in his decision making. This was corruption at its highest level.

I told you all of that, so that I can now begin to tell you the story and help you better understand, what really happened to Michael Jackson, the King of Pop.

Chapter Eight

Meetings with Michael

Meetings with Michael

In 2004, AEG was given exclusive rights to the Prince National Tour and the black promoters asked me to confront Randy Phillips of AEG about our involvement. After a conversation with him, he decided to involve us with very minimum participation. It was something that we really didn't want to accept, but we felt we had no choice, because we were so financially strained at the time, that we all needed some type of income. While in New York at Madison Square Garden for the Prince concert, I received a call from Randy Jackson and he said that his brother, Michael Jackson wanted to see me as soon as possible. Michael had asked for me to fly to Miami the following day and meet him there.

The next morning, I rose bright and early, and caught a flight to Atlanta, and later that day, about 4:00 p.m. I caught a flight to Miami. I arrived at the airport about 7:00 p.m.; I was met by Randy Jackson, and he took me over to a home where Michael was staying. When we arrived Michael opened the door. I was very glad to see him, as he was me. After hugging, and telling each other how much we missed each other, we sat down and started to talk about what each of us had been doing over the past few years. He talked about how he felt the entertainment industry had mistreated him.

He went into depth about how he felt that Steven Spielberg and David Geffen had mistreated him. I could tell he was very hurt about that. He told me he was supposed to be a partner in The DreamWorks Company, and that he wanted so badly to make a movie. Steven Spielberg told him, to find a good script, and he would be cast in the starring role. Michael said that is what he did. He said when he found a great script he sent it over to Steven Spielberg, and a couple of days later, he received a call from him. Spielberg said to him, "Michael, I have some good news, and I have some bad news. The good news is… the script you sent over was great. The bad news is that you will not be starring in the movie." Michael said that was one of the most painful days of his life. Michael knew and felt that he was being "blackballed" by the entertainment industry. He told me he did not allow his children, Prince Michael and Paris (at this particular time Blanket was a baby), to watch television, because everything that was being said about him was always negative. He said they always referred to him as "Wacko Jacko," and they were always calling him a child molester. He also said no matter what good he did in the world, it was never talked about publicly. He knew that he was disliked by the powers of the entertainment industry. I told him, "Welcome to the club." It had been that way for me, since we did the "Off The Wall Tour." I asked him if he knew I had also been "blackballed." He said he knew that he had not heard of me doing a lot of shows, like I used to. And I told him I was "blackballed" because of my association with him, and just like Michael, he apologized for that.

We stayed up until the wee hours of the morning, talking and planning. After we finished crying and laughing together, we began to make plans to tour the world. He said to me, "Rowe, after my upcoming trial…naturally I want to get my legal problems behind me. I want us to tour five continents." I told him, "We would hit America first, so this evil industry in America would not have time to set traps for us." And he agreed.

I remember, at that time Michael was in pretty good shape. He looked very good to me. He had never been a big person, but he looked healthy. The whole time I was there, he kept running out of the room to check on the kids. I saw then for the first time how great of a parent he was. I could tell the kids were not used to being around people that much, because Paris and Prince Michael jumped in and out of my lap constantly, until Michael had to run them off to bed. It was about 3:00 a.m. in the morning when I decided to turn in for the night. I told him that we would talk later.

He looked at me when I left and said, "Rowe, we are going to do this." I said, "I'm ready." When I arrived back at my hotel I was exhausted, I received a phone call from Michael. He said he wanted to make sure that I was okay, and he stated to me again, "Rowe, we are going to do this, and shake the world." Again, I said, "I'm ready."

I spoke to him almost on a daily basis up until the time he went to trial. After his trial, I did not speak to him again because he flew out of the country. When he returned to America it was two years later I believe, in 2006.

On February 14th, of 2007, I was in my kitchen fixing breakfast around 8 a.m., and I received a call. I wondered who it could be that early, but it was too early for me to talk, so I didn't answer. My phone beeped and I knew a message had been left. It was a message from Janet Jackson, Michael's sister. She said, "Rowe, this is Jan. Would you please call me as soon as possible, it's important."

I said to myself, "I wonder what she wants this time of morning." I immediately returned the call and Janet answered. She was in Atlanta, and said, "Rowe, I'm in a little trouble; my tour has been cancelled by Live Nation, and I'm obligated to my band. They have blocked their time out this summer to tour with me. And now, if I don't tour they will be missing income."

She then asked, if we could go out on tour and do twenty shows. I knew very well why Live Nation had cancelled. It was because at the time Janet was cold as ice. I did not believe that she had the drawing power to tour at that time, but I could not help but think about how much Michael and her brothers The Jacksons had done for me earlier in my career. Because of my appreciation and gratitude, I knew I would do whatever was needed to help Janet. Even if it meant losing everything I owned and possessed, I truly would have done it. It was very painful to me, when later I found her to be unappreciative of my efforts. Being a black concert promoter in the concert business, "we have always had to learn how to take lemons and make lemonade". I told her to give me a few hours to think and I would call her back later that day. I pondered over her problem all afternoon, and I came up with three scenarios. I knew Michael had returned to the states. He was now living in Las Vegas.

I later called her and said to her, "I am going to fly to Las Vegas, talk to Michael, and see if I can get him to get back with the brothers and tour. If he agrees to do that, I want you, Janet, to be the opening act." Janet loved the idea. She asked me when I was going to Las Vegas. I told her I was going in a few days, possibly Saturday. She asked if she could meet me there because she was flying back to Los Angeles, and would have her driver bring her to Las Vegas, so she could be there when I arrived that coming Saturday.

I arrived in Las Vegas that Saturday around 5:00 p.m.; we had decided that we were going to meet at her older sister, Rebbie's house before going over to Michael's. To my surprise, Jermaine, Marlon, Randy, and Jackie were also there. After a short meeting we left to go over to Michael's house about 7:00 p.m.; when we arrived we were met by Michael's security. We told them we were there to see Michael. He told us to wait one minute while he went inside to tell Michael that we were out there. When the guard returned he asked each of us to write down our names so Michael would know exactly who we were. After about fifteen minutes the security guard returned, and led us into the house. When I saw Michael I could tell he was very nervous, I truly think, he thought we were there for another reason. I noticed immediately that he was very thin. We went into the movie theater room of the house to talk.

I began to explain to Michael why we had come to see him. I told him that we wanted him to reunite with his brothers and to tour America. I told him Janet had agreed to be the opening act. I told him that I felt that this tour would be highly successful. He said that he agreed that it would be. But he said, "I just can't do it now, I have other things I am planning and working on." We stayed there for a few hours trying to persuade him. I think Janet was becoming somewhat angry with him. His final words to us were, "Maybe next year in 2008 I will be ready." To me that wasn't bad because I would need the time to prepare for a tour of this magnitude, but Janet needed to work that summer. She had committed the month of July to her band, and she needed to fulfill that commitment. I could tell that Michael was becoming irritable and we decided to leave. I knew there was a reason that he did not want to do this. And I felt if I could get him alone he would tell me. While we were walking out of the door, I turned around and asked Mike if I could speak to him in private, thinking if I could speak to him alone he would tell me his reasons for not wanting to do it. But when we went into a room for privacy, Marlon and Randy also came in, and I never received the opportunity to speak to him alone.

About two months later I flew back to Las Vegas to visit Michael again, this time hoping that I could persuade him by speaking to him alone. When I arrived I checked into the Wynn Hotel. After I changed clothes, I called Rebbie and asked her to come over and pick me up. I needed her to take me over to Michael's. She said that she would, and that she would be there in about an hour after she left The Kingdom Hall (Church). In about an hour, I met her downstairs and we proceeded to Michael's house. I asked her to let me out, and she could continue home because I wanted to be alone with Michael. I waited at the gate for about ten minutes for Michael's security guard to come down. When he arrived he said, "You have just missed Michael, let me try to get him on the phone." He called Michael and told him that I was at the house. Michael told him to ask me if I could come back tomorrow, that he would not be returning until the next morning. I said to him, that I could not come back in the morning, because I had to fly back to Atlanta for something that was important, but I would return in a few days. Michael said, "Okay".

I had already started to make other plans for Janet to go on tour. I had asked R. Kelly to tour with her and he agreed to do so. I felt this combination would be good enough for the tour to be highly successful. Janet was my main concern. While Janet and I were preparing for the tour she was rehearsing in Atlanta. She had received an offer to go to the Bahamas and perform one show at the Atlantis Hotel. She asked me if this was something she should take. I asked her "What is the deal?" When she told me, I said to her, "We must go over and do it. This will cover the expenses for the band rehearsal." We went over to the Bahamas, and while we were over there, she told me she needed to speak to me. She said to me, "Rowe, I hate to disappoint you, you have been working very hard for me, but I cannot tour with R. Kelly without a record. It will be the R. Kelly Show, and not the Janet Jackson Show, and this is something I do not want."

She said, "Let's wait until the first of the year, 2008, after I come out of the studio with at least a single, and we will tour then." I was somewhat upset because I had promised R. Kelly that we were going to tour, and I had made an agreement with him. But, I could not be angry with her because I knew that she would not be able to hold her own touring at the time with R. Kelly. Because of my commitment to R. Kelly, I was left with no choice but to tour him without Janet Jackson.

On January 1st, 2009, I was approached by a promoter from New Jersey with an incredible deal for Michael and his brothers. The deal would pay Michael alone $15 million for one performance. His brothers would receive a $1 million each for one performance. Knowing how defiant Michael was when it came to working with his brothers, I asked the promoter to do something special that maybe would persuade Michael to do this; which was to give his mother a million dollars also. The promoter agreed. I then placed a call to his mother. By this time Michael was living in Los Angeles and I did not have his new number. I asked her if she would please have Michael call me. I told her I had an incredible deal for him. She said she would do it.

I was at home the following night when I received a phone call about 9:00 o'clock. When I answered, someone was laughing, but I knew that laugh; it was Michael. He said, "Leonard Rowe." I said, "Michael Jackson." I started telling him about this incredible offer that had been presented to me. After we talked for about twenty minutes, he asked me to get on a plane and fly to Los Angeles. He wanted me to meet with the person who was handling his business at the time. That person was Dr. Tohme Tohme. Michael said, "I will have him call you immediately." About five minutes after we hung up, Dr. Tohme Tohme, called me. I told him about the offer I had for Michael.

He said that Michael told him that he had known me for a very long time, that he loved me, and told him to meet with me. I told him I would be arriving in Los Angeles the next day. He gave me his phone number and asked me to call once I arrived.

I arrived around noon LA time and gave Dr. Tohme Tohme a call. He said he was in a meeting and asked me to call him back later. I waited a few hours and called him again. He then told me he was on the phone and would call me back. He never called. The following day I called him again and I received no answer. I was beginning to think this guy was ducking me, or giving me the run around. I could not understand why, because the deal I had for Michael was like no deal I had ever seen. Most entertainers would kill to make this type of money in one day. I knew that whoever this guy was he did not have Michael's best interest at heart.

After not hearing from Dr. Tohme Tohme, I decided to call him from a different number. By this time I was getting angry about this situation. When I called him from a different number he immediately picked up. I told him I believed he was ducking my calls. I explained to him that I had flown out from Atlanta and I did not appreciate him playing games with me. I said, "Michael asked me to come and see you, and that is what I am doing. If you refuse to talk to me, I will go directly to Michael and tell him." I did not know why he was ducking such a lucrative deal for Michael, but later I found out. He asked me after that bitter conversation to meet him at his lawyer's office the following day. He assured me he was not ducking my calls, and that he had just been busy. But I knew he was lying.

The following day at about 3:00 p.m., I arrived at his attorney's office. The promoter who was making the offer also accompanied me. Dr. Tohme Tohme was there when we arrived. We presented the offer to him, but he told us that

Michael had this huge deal worth about $300 million that he had to get done first. We asked him what deal, he refused to tell us. We had heard all along that, AEG was trying to close a deal with Michael. So we left the meeting with the offer going nowhere. Dr. Tohme Tohme said he would get back in touch with us as soon as he found out about the other huge deal.

He gave us the run-around for the next two weeks. We received no information, but we stayed in LA the entire time. I finally became annoyed with the situation and I decided to call Michael. I told him how I was being treated by Dr. Tohme Tohme. Michael had also become very annoyed with this guy for some reason. Michael said that he would give Dr. Tohme Tohme a call and get back with me shortly. Michael called me a couple of days later and asked me about the deal. I told him the promoter had agreed to give his mother $1 million on top of everything else. He asked me if they would give her $2 million. I told him I did not know, but I would go and see if I could get it done. I went to the promoter and told him if he could give Michael's mother $2 million I thought we could close the deal. The promoter agreed to do so.

Later that night I received a call from Michael. It was now March 21st, 2009. When I was talking to him I noticed that he sounded like there was something on his mind. He then asked me this question, "Will you come and work with me?" He said, "I need you to oversee what AEG is doing, and to watch over my finances." He then said, "Rowe I have three children; I cannot come home from London with no money." I asked him, "What is your deal with AEG?" He said, "I do not even know what my deal is." I told him that I would be honored to do that. He said, "I don't know anything Rowe, about what is happening. I agreed to do only ten shows in London for AEG, but the next thing I knew they had sold out fifty."

The first duty that he gave me was to get in touch with Randy Phillips of AEG on Monday morning (it was then Saturday night) and go over the shows and try to arrange them in an order where they would be do-able for him. Michael said, "There is no way I can do the shows with the schedule they have in place." He asked me if I had Brother Michael's phone number. Brother Michael was head of Michael's security. I said to him, "I think I have it somewhere." He said, "Let's get him on a three-way call." I called Brother Michael and put him on the phone with Michael and myself. He told Brother Michael to get in touch with Randy Phillips and set up a meeting with him and myself as soon as possible. Brother Michael stated that he was in a public place and said that he wanted to go outside so he could understand clearly. When he went outside, Michael repeated himself again, and told Brother Michael what he wanted him to do. Brother Michael said, "Yes sir, Mr. Jackson, I will take care of it immediately." That following Monday morning, I received a call from Brother Michael around 9:00 a.m. He told me that he had spoken to Randy Phillips and Randy would be calling me around 10:00 a.m. that morning. The call never came in, so I called Randy Phillips at 10:25 a.m., and was not able to reach him. A short time after I called again and still couldn't reach him. At 12:31 p.m. I called and finally reached him. He came on the phone very arrogantly and hostile. I said, "How are you doing Randy? It's been a long time." He was very short with me. He said, "What can I do for you?" I told him that Michael had asked me to get with him, and try to rearrange the schedule where it would be more doable for him. Randy Phillips said to me, he wasn't going to do anything. He said, "We have everything under control, and I don't need to meet with you." I told him that Michael had asked me to do so. He said he was not meeting with me. I said, "Okay, thank you."

To this day Randy Phillips of AEG insists that Michael agreed to perform fifty shows, but he has never produced a contract signed by Michael to prove it. The reason he has not produced the contract is very simple, he does not have one. Every concert promoter knows that you do not put a show on sale until you have a signed contract from the artist involved. Randy Phillips knows this very well. The following day or two is when Frank DiLeo arrived in Los Angeles.

I was scheduled to visit Michael on April 14th, at his home in Beverly Hills. He asked that I come very early, around 7:00 a.m. because he had to leave for Las Vegas about 8:30 a.m. and this would give us the opportunity to talk for about an hour before he had to leave. His father Joe was now in LA, staying at the Encino family home. While I was visiting him that afternoon, I asked him, "When was the last time you saw Michael?" He replied, "I haven't seen Michael in about three years." I also asked him, "When was the last time you spoke to Michael?" He replied, "I haven't spoken to him in about three years." I said to Joe, "We are going over to Michael's house together in the morning. I will pick you up, about 6:00 a.m. be ready." You never had to worry about Joe being ready. I cannot remember one time he was ever late for anything.

I arrived at their home at 6:00 a.m. sharp, and Joe was ready and waiting. Because there was not much traffic at that time of morning, we arrived in Beverly Hills about 6:30 a.m. We went to get some coffee at my favorite breakfast restaurant in LA, Norms.

After that we continued to Michael's and arrived at 7:00 a.m. sharp. We were met by Michael's security. They were expecting us. When we arrived at the front door Michael approached us, dressed in his pajamas and wearing his reading glasses. He broke into a big smile, and I could truly tell that he was glad to see Joe. After they greeted each other, Michael asked Joe what he had been doing. They exchanged a few more words, and then Michael took us into his living room to be seated. I began to discuss with Michael the business of his personal belongings that were about to be auctioned. Joe and I had been down to the courthouse the day before to attend the hearing and we were telling Michael what we observed during that hearing. I then began talking to Michael about AEG, Randy Phillips and the London shows. I started to explain to him about some of the things they were doing that I had a problem with, such as the scalping of tickets and Michael receiving payment in U.S. currency instead of British pounds. I also asked Michael to try and separate his business as much as possible from AEG. He seemed to understand everything; he also seemed to be in full agreement.

Time was slowly approaching for Michael to start preparing to leave for Las Vegas. He then asked me, if I brought the letter that I had told him I wanted him to sign. This letter was addressed to Randy Phillips of AEG, and stated verbatim: "Dear Mr. Phillips, Please be advised that effective from the date of this letter (March 25th, 2009) that Mr. Leonard Rowe is my authorized representative in matters concerning my endeavors in the Entertainment Industry. All such matters concerning me shall be directed to Mr. Rowe, who shall act in my stead, until and unless I revoke this authorization. Please extend every courtesy to Mr. Rowe." After reading the letter Michael observed that I left off something that he told me to include. He wanted me to oversee all of his finances. He hand wrote this on the letter and signed it (See the letter on the next page). He then told me as we were leaving about a meeting that we were going to be having soon. He gave me and his father, a hug and said, "I love you both." And, then we left.

LEONARD ROWE
APPOINTMENT LETTER
FROM MICHAEL JACKSON
TO RANDY PHILLIPS

March 25, 2009

Randy Phillips
AEG
800 West Olympic Blvd., Suite 305
Los Angeles, CA 90015

Dear Mr. Phillips:

Please be advised that effective from the date of this letter, Mr. Leonard Rowe is my authorized *or financial overseer only*
representative in ~~all~~ matters concerning my endeavors in the Entertainment Industry ~~and such~~
~~other of my endeavors as he may be assigned by me~~. All such matters concerning me shall be
directed to Mr. Rowe who shall act in my stead, until and unless I revoke this authorization.
Please extend every courtesy to Mr. Rowe.

Sincerely yours, *pertaining to funnels and the O2 SHOWS in LONDON*

Michael Jackson

STATE OF CALIFORNIA

COUNTY OF LOS ANGELES

this can be revoked at any time

On March 25, 2009, before me personally came Michael Jackson, known to be to be the
individual described in and who execued the foregoing, and acknowledge to me that he executed
it.

_____

Notary Public

It was about three weeks later, approximately one month to the date. On May 15th, 2009, I received a call from Joe while I was having lunch at my hotel in the Valley, (Studio City). He said, "Rowe, you need to come quick. We are having a meeting at the Beverly Hills Hotel." I replied, "What meeting?" He said, "The meeting Michael wanted us to have with Randy Phillips, of AEG." I said, "When?" He said, "Now, get over here."

I was confused because I had not heard from Michael in about a week, and I remembered him saying we were going to have a meeting but he never mentioned when. I asked him, "Where is Michael?" He replied, "He is over here at the hotel, and he said for you to get over here now." I asked "Who is there?" He said, "Michael, Katherine, Randy Phillips, and another guy from AEG." I said to him, "I'm on my way; I'll be there in thirty minutes." I did not finish my lunch and left immediately. As I was driving through the mountains at a high rate of speed, trying to get to Beverly Hills as soon as possible, I received another call from Joe. "Rowe where are you?" he said to me. I said, "Joe, I'm coming as fast as I can. I am approximately fifteen minutes away." I could hear the urgency in his voice. He replied, "Hurry up!" Ten minutes later he called again, "Rowe, where are you?" "I am coming Joe, I am on Sunset Boulevard. I will be there in five minutes," I replied. "Hurry up," he said, "I am out in front of the hotel waiting on you."

I arrived and just as I was parking my car, Joe called again. "Where are you now, Rowe?" "I am here Joe," I replied. He said, "Meet me at the front entrance of the hotel." I said, "Okay." When I got to the front of the hotel, there stood Joe. He said, "You are holding everything up, follow me." We rushed to the room where the meeting was being held. It was in one of the bungalows located at the rear of the hotel. When we entered the room, there sat Michael, his mother, Katherine, Randy Phillips, and his business associate from AEG, Paul Gongaware. Paul was a person I had known for over thirty years, and had enormous respect for. In my presence he had always presented himself as a perfect gentleman. As we were entering, Michael stood up to greet us. We then greeted everyone else. The look on Randy Phillips' face when I entered said it all. Without saying a word, I could tell from the expression on his face that he hated to see me there. As the meeting began, my thoughts of Randy Phillips were confirmed. I had always known that he wanted to control everyone associated with Michael. His way of doing this had been with the AEG checkbook. He quickly asked me, "Who is paying you?" I replied, "That is not your concern." His face began to turn red and the meeting began.

Joe took the floor first. He began by saying to Randy Phillips, "You all are not going to cheat Michael like you have done all of his life." Joe went on to say that he felt that a lot of things that AEG was doing to Michael were wrong. Joe then looked at me, and asked me to explain what he was talking about. I said, "Okay." I knew I was going to address some sensitive and serious matters. So I thought it would be best that I make Michael aware of what I was going to be addressing. I then asked Michael if I could speak to him in private. He said, "Yes."

We went into another room to talk. I told him that I was going to discuss the scalping of tickets in London by AEG, as well as other unethical things that I felt had been done by them. I asked him if he had any objections to that. He said, "No, go right ahead."

When we returned to the room, I started asking about the scalping of tickets in London. Randy Phillips replied, "Those were not scalped tickets, they were secondary sales." I said to him, "That is just a pretty name that you have created to put on it. I have always known it to be called scalping." Believe it or not, he agreed with me, and said, "You're right."

This ticket procedure called scalping can be very lucrative for a concert promoter. When a promoter finds that he has a show in high demand he can pull a number of tickets before they go on sale. The tickets that are taken most of the time are from the first ten rows. These tickets are often referred to as premium tickets, or gold circle. For example, if a promoter pulls one thousand tickets from the gold circle and sells them through an outside broker that he controls, for $500 each over face value, he stands to profit $500,000 per show. This of course is without the artist having any knowledge of or participation in the profit. Michael's tickets were so much in demand that this was very easy for Randy Phillips and AEG to do. We had investigated and found that they had sold some of Michael's tickets for much more than $500 over the face value of the ticket. If you would do the math, and multiply just $500,000, the profit from one show, times the fifty (50) shows that Michael had sold out, you can see that AEG stood to profit millions, without Michael's knowledge. I truly believe that they viewed me as a threat to this and all other underhanded dealings they were engaging in.

When I asked Randy Phillips, "How many tickets did you scalp in London?"

His answer was, "I don't know."

I then asked him, "How much did you sell them for?"

He also said, "I don't know."

It was evident that he did not want to reveal this information to Michael or myself. I then asked Randy Phillips, "What currency is Michael going to be paid in?"

He replied, "In U.S. currency."

I said, "No. The money is being collected, in pounds. I would like for him to be paid in British pounds as well."

Once again, Randy Phillips' face turned red. The reason they would chose to pay Michael in U.S. currency, instead of pounds is because the value of the pound was worth almost 50% more than the value of U.S. currency at the time. $1 million in British pounds was equivalent to $1.4 million in U.S. Currency. By paying Michael in U.S. currency, AEG stood to profit $400,000 per show. The powers that be have always referred to African American concert promoters, as crooks, and they have spent a lot of time assassinating our character. But trust me they are the biggest crooks of all. I have always noticed that they say everyone is a crook, but them...what a joke!

As I continued talking about what I viewed as unethical business practices by AEG, Joe became highly upset to a point where Katherine had to intervene and have him sit down. Having been a promoter for the past thirty plus years, it seemed apparent that Randy Phillips and AEG were planning to take advantage of Michael in London.

There was something still nagging at me, and had been for the past few months. I had been with Michael before when he was preparing to tour. He was very much a perfectionist. He would worry you to death about every detail; he wanted everything to be perfect. But for some reason he was different this time. It was as if he knew that he would not make it to London. He didn't seem to care about any of the things that he would normally be concerned about. This was hard not to notice if you knew Michael. It was like he had an intuition or some kind of premonition that he was not going to perform in London. Soon after, Katherine (Michael's mother), Joe and I left the hotel. Outside, there were hundreds of paparazzi. It always amazed me how they seemed to always know the whereabouts of Michael. I returned to my hotel that day somewhat disappointed. I was so afraid for Michael and what he was facing. I knew without me around Randy Phillips would have no obstacles to face. I felt this would truly cause a disaster for Michael. I then remembered something that Joe had told me earlier. He said, "Rowe you can't get discouraged, you have got to hang in there and protect Michael." I knew what Joe said was true.

Chapter Nine

The People that could have saved Michael

The People That Could Have Saved Michael

I would like to begin by saying, Mrs. Katherine Jackson is a person that I love and admire. I first met her over thirty years ago. From that point on she has treated me as if I were one of her sons. But I must be as honest here as I have been throughout the writing of this book. As I look back at this whole ordeal, the one person whose actions I can't understand is Michael's mother, Katherine.

In March 2007, after I had visited Michael at his Las Vegas home, I returned to Atlanta and could not get my mind off of how Michael looked and behaved. He was very fragile, not as frail as he was in 2009, but a lot thinner than his normal body size. I called Rebbie, his older sister, and talked to her about it. I knew she could not do much of anything because at the time she had no relationship with Michael, but I called her anyway. I told her that I suspected Michael was on drugs, and that we needed to do something about it quickly. She suggested that we place a call to her mother. She asked me to put her on a three-way call. When we got Mrs. Jackson on the phone, I began to explain my concerns about Michael. I told her I believed that Michael was abusing drugs and we all needed to get together and try to get him in a treatment facility. She did not respond to me at all. I then said these words to her that I will never forget, "If you refuse to do anything, and something bad happens to Michael, you will never be able to live it down." Her response was, "You are right." But she still did not do anything to get Michael some treatment or help. I will never understand this as long as I live.

Two years later, when I arrived in Los Angeles and saw Michael he was in the worst shape ever. He weighed approximately one hundred ten to one hundred fifteen pounds. For a man five feet ten, you could imagine how he looked. He did not only look sickly to me, I knew for a fact that he was. But what really troubled me was that no one was trying to get help for him or get him into a treatment facility. I mean no one. After seeing him I first placed a call to Randy Jackson, his brother, and told him of Michael's condition. I said to him we needed to intervene and do something for your brother. He agreed and said he was on board to help. He also said to me that he had been telling this to his mother all along but she had refused to accept it. The next call I made was to Joe, Michael's father, who was now living in Las Vegas. I explained the situation to him. He said, "I will do whatever you all want me to do." Joe was also totally on board to get Michael some help. Randy later called me to talk about how we could get his mother on board with us as well. We felt that she was the most important person needed. By getting her to come on board with us, this would keep Michael from having anywhere or anyone to hide behind. We felt that if we did not have her, we would not be able to intervene and get Michael committed. We knew this would be a difficult task to say the least. Michael was her financial provider and she did not like to go against him, no matter what the circumstances may be.

I was hoping she would display the same type of tough motherly love that I had seen displayed by the mothers of Natalie Cole and Whitney Houston. Their mothers knew that they had to do something or they were going to lose their daughters. It was from their actions and tough motherly love that their children were saved.

Randy did not believe his mother would help us but I knew I had to try anyway. I told him I was going to call her and talk to her. He said to me that I needed to contact Rebbie first. He felt by both of them being Jehovah Witnesses, Rebbie would be helpful. He thought that Rebbie could persuade his mother to do the right thing by speaking to her from a Godly standpoint, convincing her that this was the right thing to do. I followed his lead and called Rebbie. I explained Michael's condition to her and told her what we were planning to do. After a lengthy conversation with her about Michael, I then asked for her cooperation in assisting us. Her response was, "I will do whatever you all want me to do." Now it was the time to place the call to Michael's mother, Katherine. I called her late that same afternoon and told her that I had seen Michael and what I thought of his condition. I explained to her how he looked and what I thought we should immediately do. I also told her it would be impossible for us to be successful in doing this without her assistance. She listened to me very attentively, but I kept noticing that she would not make a commitment to help us. We concluded the call with her telling me that she would think about it and get back in touch with me later. For the next two weeks I heard nothing from Katherine, nor did she pick up any of my calls. I knew from those actions the answer was no.

During those two to three weeks I found it to be very hard to get in touch with Michael, so I knew that Katherine had told him what I was planning to do. I really didn't care about that. I truly loved this guy, and I knew I was doing the right thing. I was trying to save his life.

Meanwhile, I kept getting phone calls from Joe, Michael's father, asking me what was going on. I told him about my conversation with Katherine. One day while talking to him he asked me to get her on a three-way call, and I did. When she came on the phone, Joe said to her in a persistent voice, "Kate, I want you to go by the hotel, pick up Rowe, and go over to Michael's house. Both of you all stay there for a few days so that you can find out and see what is going on." She said to him,

"I am not going to do that. I am not going over there and invade his privacy." Now that I look back, this was the one move that would have truly saved Michael's life. I feel so bad when I think about how we all failed Michael.

During the final months of Michael's life the person that had the most power and influence over him was Randy Phillips of AEG. In my opinion Randy Phillips had strategically inserted himself and AEG into Michael's life to a point where AEG controlled him financially. I truly believe Randy Phillips knew that Michael was in poor condition physically and financially, and he seized the opportunity to control the pop icon. AEG was virtually taking care of all of Michael's living expenses which were quite exorbitant. This gave Randy Philips and AEG the power they needed to control Michael. They took care of such huge expenses such as the $100,000 per month rental of the home he was living in, which was too much. $100,000 a month to his so-called advisor Dr. Tohme Tohme, was also too much. In addition monthly payments to Michael and his mother were being made for living expenses and to take care of his children. I feel by including Tohme Tohme on their payroll, this gave Randy Phillips and AEG complete protection from other deals that would come Michael's way. Michael would never hear about any other deals or offers. Michael had a number of offers from around the world that would have paid him $10-$15 million for each performance. AEG had Michael so financially trapped that he could not consider any of them because he knew nothing about them.

They knew that if he had knowledge of these other offers, he could have taken these offers, and freed himself from AEG's financial bond. This would have given Michael the financial freedom he needed. Tohme Tohme did his very best to make sure that these offers never reached the King of Pop. The actions of these people, in my opinion, were AWFUL!

I told Michael time and time again that Randy Phillips and AEG did not have his best interest at heart. He needed to leave them alone, and stop taking their money. He would just look at me and listen. I knew he believed what I was saying, but he was so troubled and confused that he did not know what to do. They had him caught in a web and he could not see his way out, and they knew it. I feel so bad about what they did to Michael.

One day I decided to pay a visit to Tohme Tohme's attorney, Dennis Hawk. His office was in Santa Monica, and I intentionally went over there unannounced. I was accompanied by Pat Alloco, the concert promoter from New Jersey that had made the huge offer to Michael to perform one show in the United States that would have paid him some $15 million. I knew that Hawk was not only Tohme Tohme's attorney but also a good friend of Randy Phillips. I thought by speaking to him face to face I would be able to convince him to get Randy Phillips to work with me so that we could try and get the help for Michael that he so desperately needed. I knew this was a long shot at best, but AEG, the company Randy Phillips worked for, had spent a lot of money on Michael, so I felt it would be in their best interest to help. I knew Randy Phillips resented me for no apparent reason, I might add, other than I was a person around Michael that he did not control. It didn't help that I had a personal relationship and a contract with Michael which prevented Randy Phillips and AEG from exercising total control over me. Randy Phillips resented the fact that he had to deal with me in any way, and refused to do so, even though I was properly retained by Michael to specifically handle and oversee his financial and business affairs.

A reasonably minded person would think given all that AEG

had invested in Michael and stood to gain or lose, they would have taken the appropriate measures to get Michael the treatment that he deserved and needed. Unfortunately, I was wrong. I asked Dennis Hawk to explain to Randy Phillips that with Michael in the condition that he was in, there was no way he would be able to do the shows in London if we did not get him help. I was afraid that he would not even make it to London, and as fate would have it, he didn't. What I suggested was to move the first leg of the London tour which was twenty or so shows, and put them behind the second leg, which was over six months later. This would have given Michael a chance at a six month stay in a rehab facility which he so desperately needed. I later received word from Randy Phillips telling me to "shove off".

I could not understand why Randy Phillips would be willing to take this risky chance on Michael without getting him treatment. He had to know that Michael would not be able to do these shows. By now, seeing the events that unfolded it is more clearly evident. I can only imagine the evil thoughts that Randy Phillips may have had at the time.

Randy Phillips knew he had to do something about me, when Michael asked me to come and work with him and to watch over his financials and other business affairs. This also included the shows that were scheduled for London. Michael told me that Randy Phillips had said to him that he refused to work with Leonard Rowe, and that he was calling in Frank DiLeo to manage him. If he didn't accept this, then he was going to pull the plug on everything. He knew he had Michael trapped. From that point on, Michael and I began speaking a lot less often. I received a call from Michael a day or so later and he said to me, "I want you to meet and work with Frank DiLeo."

Frank DiLeo was another person that could have been very instrumental in saving Michael's life, but it appears that he chose not to do so. In the mid 80's Frank DiLeo was an unknown record promoter. During this time he was working for Epic Records. Shortly after the release of "Thriller" Michael developed a professional relationship with DiLeo, and took a liking to him. Later Michael hired him as his manager, giving him instant fame, notoriety, and wealth. I have watched him on the Internet and television, doing interview after interview and listening to him tell lie after lie about Michael's physical health and condition. In addition to ignoring the many wrong things that were being done to Michael, I couldn't help but wonder what kind of human being Frank DiLeo was. I believe he is now being paid and compensated by Randy Phillips and AEG, who are, in my opinion, the same people that destroyed Michael. Why did Frank DiLeo need or want this type of association after all that Michael had done for him?

Frank DiLeo came to LA and was staying at the Beverly Hilton Hotel. Michael asked me to give him a call and set up a meeting with him, which I immediately did. We set the meeting for 11 a.m. the following morning. At this meeting I was hoping that he would have the same thing in mind as I did, to watch out for Michael's well-being and to make sure that Michael was not being taken advantage of in any way. I also thought this would give me the perfect opportunity to discuss Michael's health. I arrived at the hotel about 11a.m. sharp; I immediately called up to DiLeo's room to let him know that I had arrived. I told him that I was in the lobby. He said to me that he would be right down. A few minutes later he arrived. As we sat down and started to talk my hopes were shattered. It became apparent by his conversation that his loyalty was not with Michael at all, it was totally to Randy Phillips and AEG. He did not speak one word about protecting Michael or Michael's business affairs, nor did he speak about Michael's health. I was extremely disappointed. What Frank DiLeo did speak about was Randy

Phillips and AEG, and his main topic was centered on how I was going to catch AEG with the scalping of tickets in London. I had discussed this with Michael and told him that I was planning on doing something to counteract this, and make sure that he would be paid fairly for the sales of these scalped tickets. I never said what I was going to do. It became very clear to me that this guy Frank DiLeo was not working for Michael; he was clearly working for Randy Phillips and AEG. After the meeting I sent Michael a text message explaining what had transpired at the meeting, as well as my thoughts on Frank DiLeo.

Frank DiLeo was another person who could have helped in saving Michael if his heart and his loyalty had been in the right place, and that place should have been with Michael. But they clearly were not. In my opinion his loyalty was with Randy Phillips and AEG, the people that I truly feel were paying him. I felt so alone. I had no one to help me try and save Michael, no one. By this time Tohme Tohme and Michael had completely parted ways. He hated Michael, and the feeling was mutual on Michael's end. I knew better than to ask Tohme Tohme for help with Michael, mainly because he was also on AEG's payroll. Michael told me in the presence of his father at his home in Beverly Hills one morning, that he thought this guy was despicable. He also said he never wanted to see him again in his life. Michael had become very upset with Tohme Tohme for trying to auction all of his belongings. Whenever I had met with Tohme Tohme, I could honestly feel the evil spirit that he possessed. I did not know what that feeling was, but what I did know, is that he would cause destruction if he was allowed to continue in Michael's life. I was glad to see Michael get rid of him.

What I found was that the people involved in Michael's life to oversee his business affairs only cared about how they could profit from him financially. I felt that none of them cared anything about Michael as a human being. If Michael brought anyone into his life that did actually have his best interest in mind, they would do anything and everything within their power to eliminate that person, which they demonstrated in their efforts to get rid of me. Randy Phillips and Frank DiLeo claim that Michael had hired Frank DiLeo to be his manager and he was to replace me. I never heard any of this from Michael. When it came to Michael Jackson it appeared that Randy Phillips had a tendency to make things like he wanted them to be without having a signed agreement or a contract in place. I have asked numerous times where is Frank DiLeo's management contract signed by Michael. They surely would have one if that was Michael's wish, but it wasn't. In my opinion, this was an act that was forced on Michael by Randy Phillips. Michael told me himself that he would never hire Frank DiLeo again. He could have hired Frank DiLeo before he signed an agreement with me but he didn't. In my opinion, and the words of Michael, this was a move being forced on him by Randy Phillips in an effort to get rid of me.

CHAPTER TEN

THE INVESTIGATION

The Investigation

In my opinion, the investigation into Michael's death was nothing more than a complete sham. There was no investigation at all as far as I could see. I have witnessed a more thorough investigation when a dog in my neighborhood was hit by a car.

I had the opportunity to meet with the homicide investigators from the LAPD. I just happened to be at the Jacksons' home in August of 2009, when they received a visit from the LAPD homicide investigators. This was totally by accident. I can honestly say those guys did not have a clue. In my opinion they were being completely led astray by Randy Phillips and AEG. They were refusing to look at anyone other than Dr. Conrad Murray for the cause of Michael's death. I asked them, "Isn't it strange that we haven't seen any outburst of anger from Randy Phillips? Especially if you consider the fact that his company AEG was, I believe paying Dr. Murray the exorbitant amount of $150,000 per month to watch over Michael's health."

Michael did not have that kind of money at the time to pay Dr. Murray. So I ask who else could have been paying him. In my opinion there could only be one answer, and that answer could only be AEG. Randy Phillips had been trying very hard to distance himself from Dr. Murray. I told the investigators that if they would look deeply and shovel away the ashes, I truly believe when the smoke clears, they would find Randy Phillips and AEG standing there. This is my true opinion. Certain things do not make sense to me. As lawyers often say, "It just doesn't pass the smell test." I am a concert promoter myself, and have been for a number of years. If I had fifty shows sold out with Michael Jackson, and my company stood to profit an enormous amount of money from these shows, naturally I would be concerned about Michael's health. I would also do anything and everything within my power to preserve it. I truly believe AEG had agreed to pay the doctor's salary at least until Michael arrived in London. If this doctor without my knowledge went into Michael's home and administered something to him that he most certainly should not have which caused his death, I can tell you now that I would be outraged. I would be calling for this doctor to be prosecuted to the fullest extent of the law. I would want him to be put UNDER the jail. I haven't seen or heard any such actions from Randy Phillips or anyone at AEG express such anger. It just doesn't add up.

The LAPD knows that I was around Michael during the final months of his life. They also know that I had been working for him during that time. It is so strange to me that they have not tried to interview me at all since the meeting we had at the Jacksons' home, which happened by coincidence. I have said all along that this entire ordeal and the investigation into Michael's death have the lingering smell of corruption. AEG had a life insurance policy on Michael, a policy that would pay them millions of dollars upon his death. It is also strange that this insurance policy has been kept quiet. It has not been talked about publicly during the investigation, and has been completely kept out of the media. Why? I have seen time and time again, when a mysterious death has occurred and there was a large life insurance policy involved, the beneficiary of that policy always has received scrutiny and has been thoroughly looked at from the investigators standpoint until they were absolutely cleared. Not so in the case of Michael Jackson. They seem to not even want to discuss the policy, the value of the policy, or AEG involvement. It seems as though they do not want the public to know about this life insurance policy.

There were many strange occurrences leading up to Michael's death that deserve to be closely scrutinized. The people that Michael had problems with in the past, such as his former attorney, John Branca, whom Michael had vowed to never do business with again, were called in by Randy Phillips just eight days prior to Michael's death. And now Branca is heading Michael's estate. How can this be?

Michael was like many other entertainers. He did not like for his rehearsals to be filmed. This is very understandable. Artists fear that these films could be duplicated and sold without the artist's consent or control. When an artist is rehearsing, they are in a different mindset, one that they normally do not want the public to see. They sometimes say things that they do not want the public to hear, and do things they do not want the public to see or know about. Michael was persuaded to allow the filming of his rehearsals two days before his death. Why? Was it because a movie was being planned after his demise? I truly believe this was the case. While Michael was alive, his greatest wish was to star in a movie. He told me that the powers of this sometimes evil industry would not allow him to do so. Isn't it amazing that five months after his death he gets his wish? This is coming at a time when people other than his family or his children control the profits from his accomplishments. What a shame.

I also find it to be very strange that Randy Phillips would refuse to insist that Michael seek help for his addiction despite my repeated efforts to gain his cooperation in getting help for Michael. Randy Phillips insists that he did not know that Michael was using drugs. So I must ask the question why AEG would have a life insurance policy that included a drug overdose provision. Did Randy Phillips think that controlling Michael would be easier as long as he was an addict? Or did he know that by enabling Michael's drug use by employing Dr. Murray would give AEG the ultimate authority over the pop star? I truly believe so.

Randy Phillips claimed he did not know that Michael was using drugs. This happens to be the biggest tale that has been told since "Chicken Little said the sky is falling." Randy Phillips made it his business to know everything about Michael's life, down to what brand of toilet tissue he used. If he didn't know he would make sure that someone found out for him. There have been rumors of Michael's dependency on drugs for years. With all of the money that AEG had invested in him, Randy Phillips wants the public to believe that he knew nothing of his drug use. Give me a break, please. I personally sent word to Randy Phillips telling him about Michael's drug dependency and seeking his assistance to get Michael some help. I received word that he said for me to "shove off". Should this be investigated? I think so, but it hasn't been. Why?

I also find it strange that whenever someone questions the actions of Randy Phillips and or John Branca, such as Michael's sister LaToya, his father Joe, or even me, we always find our character immediately being assassinated in the media. Why? Is it because they are guilty of something? LaToya is Michael's sister and Joe is his father. Is it wrong for them to have questions about Michael's mysterious death? I say no, it's only natural. I believe they hire people who in my opinion are scum like Roger Friedman to print their garbage and tell their lies in hopes that the public will believe it. I believe this is done to divert attention away from their crime and wrongdoings, and allows them to continue stealing Michael's fortune and legacy away from his children and his family. They immediately go into a defensive mode when anyone questions the mysterious activities that surrounded Michael during the final days of his life. They begin to attack and assassinate the character of those that are inquiring. Why? They would like total silence concerning Michael's death, so what they are doing can go unnoticed and totally uninterrupted.

Whenever Joe speaks out, they get the media to talk about something that may or may not have happened over forty years ago. That is whether or not Joe spanked Michael when he was a child. They use this tactic to divert the public's attention and to create a negative opinion of his father Joe Jackson, while they quietly steal everything Michael worked so hard for all of his life. This is my opinion. His legacy should belong to his children as well as his family, and not to a bunch, who I feel are murdering thieves.

Because of what I believe to be a corrupt court system in the City of Los Angeles, John Branca and his band of pirates, in my opinion, have found it easy to accomplish their goal of controlling Michael's wealth without answering to anyone. At the same time they are keeping Michael's family and children out of the decision making process. *It is so awful what they have done to Michael.*

Chapter Eleven

Review of Michael Jackson & AEG Contract

London Contract Between
Michael Jackson & AEG

One of the hardest things for me as a concert promoter and a long-time friend of Michael Jackson to realize is just how deplorable the contract was between Michael Jackson, Michael Jackson Company, LLC and AEG. Everything in the concert promotion business is done by contract. The artist, the concert promoter, and their respective representatives get together and hash out every detail and contingency that may arise in the context of the proposed concert dates or tour.

For starters, AEG sold out fifty shows but the contract between AEG and Michael does not mention fifty shows, it speaks only of thirty-one shows. In fact, Michael told me personally that he only originally agreed to do ten shows but evidently, contractually this number was increased to thirty-one. Surely a company the size of AEG, with their in-house attorneys, that promotes hundreds of concerts every year, would surely know the simple fact that every show or leg of shows must have a signed contract by the artist before the show is put on sale. But AEG had no signed contract with Michael for fifty shows. These additional shows put increased pressure on an already sick and frail Michael Jackson, whom they knew would never want to disappoint his fans by not performing.

In reviewing the contract I was immediately struck by the total contractual binding of Michael Jackson beyond the purported shows to be scheduled for London's O2 Arena. In fact, the AEG contract with Michael Jackson doesn't end until December 31st, 2011, but Michael's London shows were to end in February 2010. In my opinion, AEG would continue to maintain a contractual stranglehold on Michael for another year and a half after the London shows had ended. Now remember that AEG was facing minimal risk because of the tremendous selling power that Michael possessed. Immediately after tickets went on sale they had millions and millions of dollars in the box office from fifty shows that had already been sold out.

So even though AEG was making ongoing advances to Michael for every possible contingency and things that he may have needed or requested; AEG was expected to be covered by the millions of dollars that would be taken in from the ticket sales. And, in the case of Michael Jackson's death, (which eventually happened) AEG was the sole beneficiary (not his children or family) on the millions of dollars worth of life insurance. Contractually AEG had the right to acquire other insurance such as cancellation insurance, non-performance coverage, and liability insurance to name just a few.

For an example of how underhanded and devious I believe the dealings were that AEG had with Michael Jackson, let's take a look at paragraph 13.1 where not only is all the insurance coverage required at Michael's expense (of which AEG is the beneficiary). In the event of death, the insurance proceeds would still not relieve Michael Jackson of the debt for advances under the AEG contract. Even though it appears AEG would have been fully paid from the life insurance and other policies, they would still be looking for additional payments from Michael's estate now that he is deceased. On top of these overreaching tactics, the contract calls for the terms and conditions to be kept strictly confidential. I truly believe this was done so that no one could see or know AEG's devious activities in dealing with Michael Jackson.

Production costs, advances for living quarters, homes in Los Angeles and Las Vegas, payments to Michael Jackson Co. LLC's manager, Dr. Tohme Tohme, and everything else was being charged to Michael Jackson as an advance to be recouped from Michael by, you guessed it, AEG.

The contract has provisions for the "term" of the contract, which defines how long the contract between the parties will be in effect. The contract also has a provision for the "territory" which defines where the geographical limitations for the performance of the contract will take place. Then there are terms and provisions for "artist compensation" and the "recoupment of advances" made by the concert promoter. When a reasonable person takes a look at the contract between Michael Jackson and AEG, you, like me, will be left with the undeniable feeling that Michael Jackson had been placed on an economic plantation with AEG as the master and overseer of all that Michael Jackson did or could do. The language of this contract is included at the end of this chapter for all to see and evaluate in order for readers to come to their own conclusions about the fairness of what I feel is a deplorable and despicable effort to manipulate and control one of the greatest entertainers the world has ever known.

I am not a lawyer so I will not try to address the many issues and concerns from the perspective of a legally trained individual. I do, however, have over thirty years experience in the entertainment business with a specific emphasis on concert promotions. That part of the business I know very well. There is little involved in the promotion of concerts by artists or entertainers, like Michael Jackson that I do not know or that I am unfamiliar with. So I address the issues and concerns that I found in the AEG contract from that perspective. With that in mind, let's take a look at the "definition section" of the AEG contract with Michael Jackson.

The first problem that I noted is in the definition of the term "advances" in that it includes "advances to the artist," Michael

Jackson as well as "production advances" which include all costs associated with production of all the dates of the tour. This problem is enhanced when you take a look at how "production costs" are defined in the contract.

In the language of this contract, "production costs" are meant to include everything from artist-related production and related costs such as "sound and lights, rigging motors, staging elements, video, pyrotechnical matters, photos and bios of the artists, the musical instruments of the band, their transportation and accommodations, passport expenses and the costs of labor unions along with the dancers, back-up singers and the costs of the tour party which includes the stage hands and related matters. Worker's Compensation, liability, and cancellation insurance policies are all considered production costs." While AEG will advance these costs, they recoup every dime from Michael Jackson's share of the proceeds of the concerts. Not one dime is paid or advanced by AEG that is not recouped from Michael Jackson. One has to wonder what risk, if any, AEG takes in this venture.

This becomes all the more outrageous when you take into account that "production costs" are normally taken from the "gross ticket sales" before any breakdown or division is done between the artists and the promoter. "Production costs" are always treated as a "show expense" and are normally never taken from the artist's share directly. The remainder should then be split between the artist and the promoter by whatever terms that were agreed upon. In this case, the contract called for a 90/10 split between Michael Jackson and AEG with Michael receiving 90% and AEG 10%. I feel AEG made this relatively simple process fuzzy and much easier for AEG to manipulate and further control Michael by including in the definition of "advances" to include "both artist advance" and "advances for production costs."

Now it was widely publicized throughout the world that the "This Is It" Tour was for a certain number of shows to be played at London's O2 Arena. However, the definition of the "term of the contract" means from the date the contract was executed -- January 26th, 2009 through December 31st, 2011. That is a long time to keep someone like Michael Jackson contractually bound when the London shows were supposed to have taken place between July 8th, 2009, and February 24th, 2010. Why would AEG maintain this long of a period of what appears to be *contractual enslavement* of Michael Jackson for almost two years after the London dates were to have been played and completed?

If this is not bad enough, the AEG contract allows AEG to keep Michael Jackson's money made from the tour for an extra sixty days before they had to settle up and pay him for the services he had already rendered. Now, it has been my experience that African Americans have always been treated differently in this business, but from the shows and tours that I have done over the past thirty years, it has always been customary for an artist to be paid every night after their show or in the case of a tour, on Monday morning for their past weeks' performances. Why would AEG's contract allow them to hold Michael Jackson's money for two extra months knowing how critical his financial condition was at the time? This is unheard of, and AEG knew that I would not have allowed this abuse to happen on my watch.

Section 4 of the AEG/Michael Jackson contract defines the tricky subject of "artist's compensation." Michael Jackson's contract with AEG calls for him to receive 90% of the "net pool revenue." What is "net pool revenue?" Well, that term is defined as "pool revenue" that is generated during the "term" minus the expenses of the "pool" during the "term" on a fully cross-collateralized basis. To make it simple so you can understand, let's take the "gross pool revenue" taken in from a concert, let's say the "gross pool revenue" is $1 million and the expenses for that concert are $300,000, which leaves $700,000 as the "net pool revenue." "Pool revenue" is extensively defined to include "gross ticket proceeds received by the promoter" and is actually called "adjusted gross ticket revenue." It also includes specific ticket rebates, refunds, or expense savings that the promoter receives. Now the contract in my opinion views them, the artist and the artist's company, as *"potential participants"* in the receipt of *"adjusted gross ticket revenue."* However, in my opinion Michael Jackson and his company, Michael Jackson Company, LLC, would have never seen a single cent of ticket sales revenue, because Michael Jackson and his company were in my opinion only viewed as *"potential participants,"* whether or not it was called *"adjusted gross ticket revenue"* or simply the total amount of tickets sold. I believe every dime would have gone from Ticketmaster to AEG, and not to Michael Jackson or Michael Jackson Company, LLC, until AEG decided, two months later, what, if anything, they were going to pay Michael Jackson. My belief after reviewing this contract is that they planned to pay him NOTHING.

Another interesting term that is specifically defined in the AEG contract with Michael Jackson is "artist's net tour income". This is defined as the "contingent compensation minus the amounts of production costs, plus the portion of the contingent compensation that includes Merchandise Revenue (which is separately defined)." It also includes "Net Show Related Broadcast/Recording Revenue (which is also separately defined)."

So from the outset, while the AEG contract with Michael Jackson sets forth a 90% payout to Michael of the "net pool revenue" which is called "contingent compensation," it is subject to all the production costs and other expenses which are charged directly to Michael Jackson as part of the advances paid by AEG, in my opinion to "economically enslave" Michael. "Pool expenses" and "production costs" are two areas where AEG can, and in my opinion, planned to "milk" Michael Jackson for hundreds of thousands of dollars, because what happens is that each and every thing that is covered under those terms are treated as an "advance," all of which are charged directly to, you guessed it, Michael Jackson.

Now there is one aspect of "production costs" that sticks in my craw, in a very unbelievable way. That aspect is the sideline agreement that AEG had with Dr. Tohme Tohme, Michael Jackson's business overseer. Dr. Tohme Tohme was responsible for running The Michael Jackson Company, LLC, at the time the London contract was executed. Take a look at paragraph 6.8 of the AEG contract with Michael Jackson, which is titled "Management Agency and Legal Costs."

For reasons that are presently unknown, AEG agreed to pay Dr. Tohme Tohme $100,000 per month pursuant "to the terms of a separate agreement with TT International, LLC." This is Dr. Tohme Tohme's personal company. Now why is it that AEG would be contracting individually with the person that is charged with running the operations of Michael Jackson's company and paying that person, Dr. Tohme Tohme, $100,000 per month? What in the world was Dr. Tohme Tohme doing for this amount of money every month for AEG? And was his loyalty to Michael Jackson compromised by virtue of the sideline agreement of his personal company, TT International, with AEG? It doesn't take a rocket scientist to see that something was wrong with this situation.

And if that was not enough to turn your stomach, the $100,000 that AEG contracted to pay Dr. Tohme Tohme was also considered an "advance" against Michael Jackson's "contingent compensation." Now how fair is that? In my opinion it appears that Dr. Tohme Tohme sold Michael Jackson out to AEG, and then AEG pays Dr. Tohme Tohme for doing so, leaving poor Michael Jackson stuck with the bill. It is nothing short of despicable and deplorable the way that these people mistreated Michael Jackson.

Unknown to Michael Jackson, this money, paid to TT International, LLC for Dr. Tohme Tohme by AEG was, in my opinion, to block and conceal all other offers that would come Michael Jackson's way. By this being done AEG would be free of competition so that the economic slavery and servitude that AEG had contractually subjected Michael to would not be interfered with in any way. Such offers as the one made by AllGood Entertainment that would have paid Michael some $15 million for one show. The litigation in this matter against AEG is currently ongoing. Offers such as these would have freed Michael from the financial bondage that he was under with AEG.

In hindsight, it was easy for them to do this because Michael Jackson was in such bad shape emotionally, physically, and psychologically due to his extensive use of narcotic drugs for pain and other medical conditions taken for past injuries. So when your body is dependent on drugs and your financial situation is critical and someone places a doctor in your home to provide you with the narcotics that you crave, it is not difficult for them whom you have entrusted to handle your affairs to take advantage of you. However, in reality, you are being manipulated by this person or persons for their own benefit and the benefit of their co-conspirators. In this case, I truly feel this is what happened to Michael by Dr. Tohme Tohme and AEG. Conflicts of interest are not just reserved for lawyers; they are also to be reserved and respected by anyone when doing business.

As pointed out earlier, concert promoters such as AEG are to facilitate the needs of the artist and ensure that the venue, productions costs, insurance, ticket sales, advertising, and all other aspects of the tour or the concert are handled so that things flow smoothly when the lights go on and the curtain goes up. In the case of AEG and Michael Jackson, I believe everything needed for the fifty shows in London was facilitated in the final instance by Michael Jackson solely at his cost and expense. In my thirty plus years as a concert promoter I have never seen a contract with any artist as deplorable as this one.

I feel AEG, in a very real sense, takes no risk in any way other than by pouring money and more money into all of the various things and entities that were connected to Michael Jackson. It is apparent that AEG became nothing more than a financial "overseer" of Michael Jackson, whom, in my opinion, they literally enslaved through the contract that I believe Michael was tricked and manipulated into signing.

Just take a look at the section of the contract that addresses *"artist compensation."* I pointed out to you previously that Michael Jackson is thought to be entitled to 90% of the "net pool revenue but this 90% is cross-collateralized and referred to as *"contingent compensation."* It's contingent because something else has to take place before it is paid out. So the first question becomes, contingent upon what?

But before we try to answer that question, let's take a look at what Michael gets 90% of. Remember, the AEG contract with Michael states that he gets 90% of the "net pool revenue" which is defined as "pool revenue generated during the 'Term' less 'Pool Expenses' incurred during the 'Term', on a fully cross-collateralized basis." So, in order to really see what Michael Jackson's 90% is, in real-time dollars, we have to take a close look at what "pool revenue" and "pool expenses" consist of.

Earlier we discussed "adjusted gross ticket revenue," interest on income received by the tour, proceeds from shows that were sold off by the promoter to another promoter, "merchandise revenue," "broadcast and recording-related revenue," and "fan club revenue," all of which come into the concept of "pool revenue".

"Pool expenses" were spoken about earlier and it includes all *"customary and mutually approved costs for the shows that are incurred by AEG, the Promoter,"* which controls the O2 Arena in London. These expenses include venue rental, net advertising, marketing material, public liability insurance, security, ticketing costs (which probably include the printing of tickets and related matters), local staff, venue staff, power in the venue, and other venue expenses involving pre-rigs, and roof rental. Roof rental is related to outdoor shows, but they didn't charge Michael these expenses, which AEG had the right to sell off to a third party promoter. None of this has emerged since Michael's death; so it is probably safe to assume that no shows were sold off to a third party promoter. AEG had also purchased cancellation insurance. This means that AEG would still get paid no matter what happens, as it appears that they have.

"Production costs" were also touched upon when we discussed how sickening it was for AEG to pay Michael Jackson's manager, Dr. Tohme Tohme, $100,000 per month under a separate contract with TT International, LLC, for his services. So when one includes all the "pool expenses" and "production costs" in conjunction with the "artist's advances," which AEG is contractually allowed to recoup from the artist, when all is said and done, Michael Jackson's 90% "contingent compensation" would be eaten up in all of the "pool expenses," "production costs," and "advances" such that in my opinion Michael Jackson would end up with very little or, heaven forbid, owing AEG money. One would feel when viewing this contract that Randy Phillips and AEG could be very generous. But what one must understand is that, it appears they had no care or concern about paying exorbitant salaries to anyone because all that they paid out would be "recouped" from Michael. And that, my friend, is where the reality of economic slavery comes into full view. Because not only must Michael stay on tour around the world whenever and wherever AEG requires, but he must do so until every dollar advanced by AEG is recouped.

In the definition section of the contract, Paragraph 14 of Exhibit A, which defines the "term," AEG has the right to make Michael perform, even after December 31st, 2011, when the "term" would end in order to "recoup 100% of all advance payments" that AEG had made to Michael long after the fifty shows had ended in London.

Now in an attempt to be fair here, AEG would argue that Michael had the right to buy out his obligations under the contract with AEG. But not until the expiration of the initial term of the contract which expires on December 31st, 2011, which AEG could extend at its sole discretion with written notice to TT International. Until December 31st of the next year, Michael Jackson is caught in this contractual spider web that sucked up all of his blood, sweat, and tears because Michael Jackson wanted to do one thing and one thing only, please his worldwide adoring fan base with his music and showmanship. Other than the care for his children and his family, nothing else mattered to Michael.

The AEG contract with Michael was overseen on Michael's behalf, by Attorney Dennis J. Hawk, who was supposed to be the lawyer for the Michael Jackson Company, LLC. In other words, he was Michael's lawyer, or so you would be led to believe, because in reality, Dennis J. Hawk, like Dr. Tohme Tohme, in my opinion, was being paid by AEG. So while we are going through this contract, we must bear in mind that Michael Jackson was placed in this economic strait-jacket by people that he had hired and was supposed to be able to trust to look after his best interests. Instead, all of the people that were responsible for keeping Michael Jackson protected and insulated from abuse by predators and parasites in the entertainment industry were the very same people who were in complicity and collusion with AEG and the enemies of Michael Jackson. Michael was defenseless against the numerous lies and evil deceptions as they all went about the business of carving out their own little niche of Michael Jackson's soul at Michael Jackson's expense. I told Michael, on numerous occasions, that these people "meant him no good".

Taking advantage of Michael was very easy for them to do because of his condition. His health was poor, his body's addiction was very prevalent, his financial condition at the time was deplorable, and in my opinion, AEG knew it all, along with those who helped them to perpetrate this hoax on Michael Jackson and his fans around the world. These people exploited Michael Jackson's brand, his music, his showmanship, and his extraordinary talent which was unmatched in history, with no compassion or sensitivity for Michael.

And through the images of the Michael Jackson that we remember, AEG sold out fifty shows in an arena, that AEG controls, months before Michael was ever scheduled to hit the stage for show number one. Money from the sale of the tickets had already been received and a life insurance policy had also been acquired so at this point, AEG was financially safe.

Another part of the AEG contract that sticks out like a sore thumb is the provision that comes after the section on "contingent compensation." We discussed how utterly deplorable that section of the contract was to Michael Jackson, but what's worse is the section addressing "advances of contingent compensation." There was an initial advance of $5 million. Now, you would think that $5 million is a lot of money and it is. But Michael Jackson didn't see $5 million of the initial advance because AEG sent three million of it to another company, 2 Seas Records, LLC, supposedly to settle a debt owed by Michael Jackson. So after the $3 million went somewhere else, Michael Jackson got $2 million as his initial advance. Remember now, all advances are to be recouped by AEG before Michael Jackson gets to his 90% of "contingent compensation." But in addition to the "initial artist advance," AEG made advances to cover Michael Jackson's home rental at the rate of $100,000 per month or $1.2 million per year, and all related expenses. And that is just on one home in Beverly Hills, California, the home where he ultimately died.

I was told by Michael that AEG found the home and that they had contracted the home for him. Surely they are more business savvy than to pay $100,000 per month to rent, rather than to buy, a home. Would Randy Phillips have made this type of business arrangement for himself? I would not bet on it. When Michael told me this, I thought it was simply deplorable knowing that Michael Jackson had no concept of money. I felt yet again that he was being taken advantage of by AEG.

But the advances don't stop there. Michael Jackson was also allowed an advance to purchase a home in Las Vegas and this was for $15 million. This advance was "conditional" upon

Michael Jackson executing a promissory note which is attached to the AEG contract with Michael Jackson in the amount of $6.2 million. All of this, I truly believe, was designed for one purpose and one purpose only, to increase Michael's debt to AEG so that eventually they could take control of all Michael Jackson's remaining assets which included his priceless catalogue. I had told Michael on numerous occasions that Randy Phillips presented himself as the second coming of "Mother Theresa". But I begged Michael not to believe it, because he was anything but that.

The interesting thing about the promissory note that Michael Jackson was required to execute for the advances on the Las Vegas home is that it bears no interest rate unless the full principal amount that is owed is not paid within five business days after the maturity date, which is supposed to be defined further in the promissory note. Now there is no section in the promissory note that explicitly defines maturity date. What AEG did was define maturity date through the term of the note in the following manner:

"The term of this Note shall be from the date of this Note through and including the earlier of (a) six months after the last Show of the first leg of the Tour under the Tour Agreement (defined below) but in no event later than December 31st, 2009 or (b) six months after Promoter makes a written request for such payment, if ever, in accordance with Paragraph 4.2.5 of the Tour Agreement (defined below), (such earlier date shall be referred to as the "Maturity Date".), at which time all unpaid principal shall be due. The parties may renew the term and extend the Maturity Date by signing a written modification of this Note extending such dates, and shall do so if required by the terms of the Tour Agreement."

This promissory note from Michael Jackson Company, LLC and Michael Jackson, the artist, required Michael to pay the principal amount of the note, in full on the maturity date as defined above to be about six months after the first leg of the tour in London, but not later than December 31st, 2009 (whichever comes first), or six months after a written request is received from AEG by Michael Jackson or his company. However, AEG gets really slick here in this promissory note, because the entire note is collateralized not by Michael Jackson the artist, but by Michael Jackson Company, LLC. Why is this you may wonder? More than likely it is because Michael Jackson's business holdings, which would include his publishing rights and catalogue, are owned by Michael Jackson Company, LLC and not Michael Jackson, the individual artist. So if the promissory note is for any reason not paid or defaulted upon, the assets of the Michael Jackson Company, LLC get forked over to AEG. In other words, owning Michael Jackson Company, LLC and/or its assets, means owning Michael Jackson.

If I were a betting man, I would wager money that nothing this deplorable, overreaching, and unfair would ever be presented to Barbra Streisand, Bono of U2, Rod Stewart, or any other top white artist in the world. But in my opinion, AEG and its band of thieves had no problems whatsoever doing these terrible contractually binding things to Michael Jackson whom I believe they knew at the time was incompetent to make these kind of business decisions.

These were just some of the things that AEG and others wanted to prevent me from doing for my friend Michael. I truly believe they knew I would expose them and their unfair undertakings that were being advanced in Michael's name, but was clearly not in Michael's best interest. It was truly awful, in my humble opinion, what these people did to my friend, Michael Jackson.

Just so that we are all clear on what collateral is owned by the Michael Jackson Company, LLC, let's take a quick look at what and how AEG defined and collateralized the promissory note. It quotes, in Exhibit C, page two, as follows: "To secure the faithful and timely performance of each Maker's obligations hereunder and each Maker's obligations under the Artist Agreement, and all extensions, modifications, substitutions, replacements and renewals... "Artistco (which is the Michael Jackson Company, LLC)," hereby assigns and grants to Holder, (AEG) a security interest in "Artistco's rights," title and interest in, to, and under the following properties, assets and rights, wherever located, whether now owned or hereafter acquired or arising, and all proceeds and products thereof (all of same being hereinafter referred to collectively as, the "Collateral"): contract rights, the right to the payment of money in which "Artistco" has an interest, insurance claims and proceeds, commercial tort claims, securities and all other investment property, and all general intangibles (including all accounts receivables and payment intangibles). "Artistco" shall cooperate in Holder's efforts to perfect the security interest granted to Holder hereunder. To the extent allowed by law, "Artistco" hereby irrevocably appoints Holder (which is AEG), acting singly, as "Artistco's" attorney-in-fact, with full authority in the place and stead of "Artistco" and in the name of "Artistco," or otherwise, in Holders discretion, if a Default shall have occurred and be continuing, to take any action and to execute any instrument that Holder may deem necessary or advisable to accomplish the purposes of this agreement..."

Now the AEG Contract indicates that "ARTIST IS NOT PLEDGING ANY COLLATERAL". Let me explain to you this trickery. Why should he, when the entire ownership interest of everything that Michael Jackson's company owned, is pledged to AEG per the contract? In my opinion, AEG ought to be ashamed of what they did to Michael. In other words, should Michael default, AEG would own Michael Jackson's company which includes his publishing rights, investment holdings, his memorabilia, and his many Grammy Awards. Per this contractual language, Michael actually was duped into turning over all of his company's assets to AEG. They would own it under the terms of the promissory note that was executed to secure advances under the Artist Tour Agreement with AEG. I have never seen anything this horrible be put upon any artist in history, since I have been in the entertainment industry for some thirty plus years. But, in my opinion, AEG did these things and worse to Michael Jackson. AEG even had contingencies against Michael Jackson and/or his company going bankrupt.

Let me explain. For example, say that Michael Jackson discovered, as he would have if I had remained at his side, like he wanted, that the terms and conditions of either the promissory note for the Las Vegas home acquisition, or the agreement discussed here with AEG were not in his best interest. And, supposing he found that his liabilities were deemed greater than his assets. If he wanted to change it or get out of the contract altogether, Michael could have decided to file for bankruptcy protection under the law, which he had a legal right to do. But, in this contract, if Michael decided to file bankruptcy he would then lose his entire fortune to AEG.

Any other normal citizen could file bankruptcy and stop his or her creditors from coming after them and taking their property until things were sorted out in the bankruptcy proceedings. Not Michael Jackson. Filing for bankruptcy protection is considered, under the terms of this promissory note, an "event of default" which allows the Holder (AEG) to do all sorts of things without notice to Michael Jackson.

You may ask what kind of things? Without "presentment," "demand," "notice of any kind," all of which they made Michael Jackson "waive," AEG has the right, under this deplorable agreement, to declare the entire outstanding balance of principal and interest due and payable immediately. And get this, AEG gets to "exercise or enforce its rights to its Collateral." That means AEG gets to take Michael Jackson's company, publishing and property, which includes the house that he bought for his mother, and keep it for themselves. From what I have learned over the years about Randy Phillips and AEG, they most certainly would have done this. This is my opinion.

So for a $6.2 million promissory note, (*which Michael Jackson would have surely defaulted on because of poor health and addiction to medication which I truly feel that AEG was fully aware of*), AEG gets to take the entire Michael Jackson catalogue, which is now valued at around $3 billion. Not to mention all of Michael Jackson's publishing rights which include the song book of the Beatles, one-half of Sony/ATV, and many other artists whom Michael Jackson invested in. Ladies and gentlemen, you do not understand how awful this contract was for Michael Jackson.

Dennis Hawk, the attorney that oversaw this deplorable contract on Michael's behalf, should, in my opinion, be disbarred and not allowed to practice law ever again. AEG or anyone in their right mind would not have presented such a one-sided contract to Paul McCartney, Barbra Streisand, Celine Dion, or any other artist. It is so awful what they have done to Michael.

But they slammed this down the throat of a poor and ailing Michael Jackson. And everybody that Michael had hired to protect him from these unseemly elements in the entertainment industry failed him miserably. They did not do anything which Michael had hired or retained them for. And that goes doubly and especially for Dr. Tohme Tohme and Dennis Hawk, who was supposed to have been the attorney that Michael Jackson was relying on to make sure that he was not taken advantage of. This attorney, Dennis Hawk, was rumored to be good friends with Randy Phillips. In fact, after I spoke to Dennis Hawk on several occasions and he told me that he was overseeing the contract on Michael's behalf, I had to wonder whose interests he was really representing. I truly believe that AEG was paying Dennis Hawk for his services in drafting the deplorable contract that we are discussing right now. How Dennis Hawk could hold himself out as Michael Jackson's lawyer or the attorney for the Michael Jackson Company, LLC, while actively working in concert with AEG, is far beyond my ability to comprehend.

In conclusion, the promissory note was just another aspect of the tools of economic enslavement that AEG had subjected Michael Jackson to in the months leading up to his untimely demise. It was a shame, a disgrace, and nothing short of a national tragedy that this was allowed to happen in the twenty-first century here in America.

What I perceive to be the greed of AEG and its band of thieves did not end with the ironclad grip around Michael Jackson's throat by way of this contract. AEG controlled everything that went on around Michael Jackson. They claimed to not have hired or to have been responsible for the actions of Dr. Conrad Murray, whose first two calls on that fateful day in June of last year were not to 911 as one would think, but to at least two other people. I can't help but wonder who those other two people were. We will come back to this matter later. I personally know, for a fact, that AEG maintained control of everything and everybody that had any access to Michael, other than me.

Let's continue here with Section 4.2.4 of the AEG/Michael Jackson contract. It provides that AEG may execute yet another Promissory Note "in a form substantially similar" to the one that we discussed above. This would also be against "Artistco's future entitlement to contingent compensation."

Now, one could reasonably question why someone would let Michael Jackson be taken advantage of in this manner. AEG had Michael Jackson "strung out" on "artist advances" which included: (1) the initial artist advance, (2) the interim artists advances, (3) the Las Vegas Residence Advance, (4) the Home Rental Advances, and (5) each additional artist advance. And, all of them are "recouped", along with all other show expenses, by AEG from the 90% of "contingent compensation" that Michael Jackson is supposed to be entitled to under the terms and conditions of this lopsided contract. Why would Dr. Tohme Tohme and Dennis Hawk advise Michael Jackson to enter into a contract that was this deplorable with AEG? I can tell you why. It's like Michael told me on numerous occasions "Rowe, they want my catalogue". This is my opinion.

The terms "malpractice" and "breach of fiduciary duty," I feel, did not ever come into play with this lawyer and so-called business manager. I wholeheartedly believe Michael Jackson was deceived and taken advantage of by these people for AEG. People, this is so unethical that it should be unlawful. These terms are mild compared to what they have done to Michael.

Michael Joseph Jackson, the musical equivalent of the "light of the world" was betrayed and destroyed by those closest to him and the terms and conditions of this unfair and unconscionable contract clearly shows how they did what they did and why. The money that has been made off of Michael Jackson, his music, his legacy, the movies, books, and re-issues of his timeless musical talents have brought in untold hundreds of millions of dollars in the past year since his death. Who controls this money? Not his children, or his family. But Michael Jackson's estate, which is being run by, in my opinion, yet another conniving, high class thief, John Branca, Michael's former attorney (whom he had fired because Michael suspected him of embezzlement). When all is said and done, many unfortunate things have happened. When you look at it from a financial standpoint, AEG came out smelling like a rose. I can't help but wonder was AEG just lucky, or was all of this purposely planned?

Let's talk again about "secondary tickets sales" which are specifically mentioned in the contract. "Secondary sales" are nothing more than a pretty name for ticket scalping. The way this works is that the promoter can take say, two thousand tickets from each show, generally from the first ten to fifteen rows of seats which are normally the best seats in the house and closest to the stage. The promoter hands these tickets over to a ticket broker that the promoter controls. Then, the ticket broker sells those tickets to wealthy patrons for hundreds and sometimes thousands of dollars over the regular price of the ticket. What the promoter does then is put the standard price for each ticket, which in this case was around $100, back into the pool and the artist would never know the difference and would never see the overpayment money generated by this ticket scalping practice. In this case, this would have amounted to millions and millions of dollars that Michael never would have received if I was not present.

Now imagine how one would feel as an artist, when they see the report that tickets for every show have sold out, but they are unknowingly getting paid on the face value of the ticket, which is the $100 regular ticket price. But, in reality the promoter has made millions of dollars that the artist, in this case, Michael Jackson, would have never known anything about.

When one does the math, it becomes relatively easy to compute the loss that Michael Jackson would have suffered based solely in my opinion, on the unscrupulous, dishonest methods and practices of his concert promoter, AEG. I believe AEG would have never told Michael Jackson a single word about these practices until I raised the issue in a meeting with Michael and Randy Phillips on May 15th, 2009, at the Beverly Hills Hotel. Michael Jackson's mother and father were also present at this meeting when this topic was addressed by me.

Legally speaking, in most cases, overpayment of these tickets is not guaranteed for refund in case of cancellation. The face value of the ticket is all that is normally required for purposes of refunds. This creates an enormous profit for the concert promoter or the person who serves as the ticket scalper. Randy Phillips of AEG did not like the fact that I was exposing industry insider practices and procedures to Michael Jackson and his parents. But this is precisely what Michael Jackson hired me to do, to watch over his business and financial affairs. To say that this created problems for AEG and those who did not have Michael's best interest at heart would be a tremendous understatement. And this is the main reason why they wanted me out of the way and to simply disappear.

The more that I think about it, the more disappointed I become. Never, in my thirty-five year career in the entertainment industry have I witnessed a star of the caliber and magnitude of Michael Jackson be so thoroughly taken advantage of by those around him who were entrusted with his best interest and well-being. I feel that everyone Michael thought was in his corner betrayed him, with the exception of certain members of his family and me. It is one of the primary reasons that AEG, John Branca, Dr. Tohme Tohme, Frank DiLeo, and others wanted to make sure that I was gone. They knew that I would not sit idly by and tolerate the unfair games that they were playing on Michael Jackson. And for once they were right.

There are a lot of different clauses and provisions in contracts like the one that AEG had with Michael Jackson. As the old saying goes, "the devil is in the details." It doesn't take long for the "devil" to be found in the details of the contract between AEG and Michael Jackson. Sometimes you can spot a problem right away. Others are so deeply hidden in the language of the contract, that when taken by itself sounds like the clause might be harmless. However when taken in conjunction with other clauses, it becomes totally unacceptable in the context of other provisions of the contract. In my opinion, this is how they were manipulating and tricking Michael Jackson.

For example, in the promissory note that is merely an attachment or an exhibit to the primary contract, you find the following language on page two, in bold letters:

"SECURITY AGREEMENT -- COLLATERAL OWNED BY ARTISCO ONLY -- ARTIST IS NOT PLEDGING ANY COLLATERAL" (What a joke!)

Now at first glance you would think that provision is okay. Right? This is because Michael Jackson is not pledging any collateral for the promissory note, which incidentally, was for $6.2 million to buy the Las Vegas home. What this means, ladies and gentlemen, is that AEG owns Michael Jackson Company, LLC for a mere $6.2 million as collateral for that amount. Now remember the language says no "collateral" is "pledged by the artist," meaning Michael Jackson. But the AEG contract with Michael Jackson includes all of the contract rights that Michael Jackson Company, LLC is party to as part of the collateral, which includes the AEG contract with Michael Jackson the artist.

Now if that wasn't a clever and deceitful tactic, you had better open your eyes so that you can clearly see what was being done in broad daylight and right under everybody's nose. In my opinion, AEG had enslaved Michael Jackson, while trying to make it look like they were doing him a favor. I truly feel they were engaged in one of the most despicable thefts of intellectual property and talent the world has ever seen. All of Michael Jackson's publishing holdings and most of his personal belongings were a part of the Michael Jackson Company, LLC. Poor Michael did not own much of anything in his personal name.

So that means, unfortunately, that the executor's of his estate, whom I believe are fraudulent are, in my opinion, in collusion with AEG, who continues to claim its contractual rights after Michael's death.

AEG is a concert promotion company. That is the duty that they were serving for Michael Jackson on his London concert tour. Being a concert promoter myself, I can't help but ask the question, why are AEG and Randy Phillips still involved in Michael Jackson's business along with his estate? They were just the concert promoter of his London shows. When Elvis Presley died, no concert promoter was involved with his estate. When John Lennon passed away, no concert promoter was involved with his estate. Why is it that AEG appears to have a permanent interest and involvement in Michael Jackson's estate? This just doesn't pass the smell test.

The more you look at what I perceive to be devious dealings by AEG, the more important and essential it was that AEG get rid of me. They knew in no uncertain terms that I would never stand for any of this nonsense they were pulling on Michael. Never in all of my years in the entertainment business, have I ever seen a concert promoter allowed to dictate to an artist who the artist has to hire or fire to oversee their personal management and/or business affairs. But AEG saw it differently when it came to Michael Jackson and me. I truly believe, it became absolutely essential for AEG to have me totally removed from around Michael Jackson in order for their evil plans to work and be effective.

I was told by Michael Jackson that Randy Phillips had called him for a mysterious meeting. At this meeting, Michael said he was told that AEG refused to work with Leonard Rowe, and that he had to get rid of me. They were calling in Frank DiLeo to manage him and take my place. If Michael did not agree they were going to pull the plug on everything and demand payment of all the advance money that AEG had provided him. They knew that they had Michael Jackson where they wanted him. *How despicable can you be?* They often publicize that Joe Jackson, Michael's father, is trying to profit off of Michael Jackson's death. But ladies and gentlemen, let's be for real; who is *really* profiting from the death of Michael Jackson? The answer is perfectly clear, and it is not Joe Jackson. If John Branca's son had died, would he allow someone to falsely come in and take control over his son's estate which includes his assets and accomplishments? Certainly not. Nor would Branca's character be questioned and constantly assassinated in the media as they are doing to Joe Jackson, Michael's father.

As of now, I feel they have accomplished their goal to strip Michael Jackson of everything that he has worked his entire life to accomplish. It appears to me that AEG, John Branca, and their band of thieves are controlling everything that Michael Jackson worked so hard for. Neither his children nor his family have final say over Michael's assets. It is so awful what they have done to Michael Jackson, the undisputed King of Pop.

I truly hope that the world is not tricked or bamboozled by what I perceive to be the most despicable act ever committed in my lifetime.

Chapter Twelve

Copy of the Actual Michael Jackson & AEG Contract

January 26, 2009

MICHAEL JACKSON

The Michael Jackson Company, LLC

██████████████████

██████████████████

██████████

██████████

Attn: Dr. Tohme Tohme

Dear Dr. Tohme:

     This agreement (this "Agreement") is entered between AEG Live, LLC dba Concerts West, a Delaware limited liability company ("Promoter"), on the one hand, and The Michael Jackson Company, LLC, a Delaware limited liability company, (Federal Employer Identification Number ████████) ("Artistco") furnishing the services of Michael Jackson ("Artist") and the Artist, on the other hand, as follows:

1.   **Definitions.** The capitalized terms contained herein shall have the meaning ascribed to such terms herein and/or in the attached Exhibit A, as applicable.

2.   **Promoter's Rights.** Artistco and Artist hereby grant Concerts West the following rights during the Term and throughout the Territory: (a) the exclusive right to promote the Shows in the Territory, (b) the exclusive right to manufacture and sell, and/or arrange for others to manufacture and sell mutually-approved Artist Merchandise at each of the Shows and on the official website of the Artist (www.michaeljackson.com) or such other website identified by Artistco in the event it selects another URL for the Artist's official website , (c) the right to solicit mutually-approved Sponsors to any and all Shows and to execute Sponsorship Agreements; and (d) the non-exclusive right to use the Artist's name and approved likeness in connection with Promoter's exercise of any of the foregoing rights. Promoter will be allowed to sell off Shows; provided that Promoter shall remain primarily responsible for its obligations hereunder in connection with such Shows, unless otherwise agreed by Artistco. Artist shall not engage in any live performances in the Territory during the Term except that Artist may engage in the following live performances during the Term and in the Territory so long as they do not interfere with the Artist's services in connection with the Tour or negatively impact ticket sales in connection with the Shows: (i) promotional and private shows where tickets are not sold or advertised to the general public; (ii) television and award shows; (iii) charity and radio shows; and (iv) other mutually agreed upon shows.

3.   **Itinerary of Shows.** Artistco and Promoter shall reasonably cooperate with each other in an effort to arrive at mutually approved itineraries for each leg of Shows during the Term; provided however, it shall be unreasonable for Artistco to withhold or qualify its approval of any itinerary or amended itinerary proposed by Promoter if the date range of such itinerary does not exceed ten (10) weeks, the frequency of Shows within such itinerary does not exceed one Show per day and 3.5 Shows

per seven-day period, on average, and the locations of the proposed venues are in metropolitan areas. Artistco hereby pre-approves up to thirty one (31) Shows, or such other greater number as agreed by Artistco and Promoter, at the O2 Arena in London, England between July 26 and September 30, 2009. Subject to the foregoing, Promoter and Artistco shall mutually agree on the number of legs of Shows and the number of Shows in each leg during the Term, and Artistco shall supply a first class performance of Artist in accordance with this Agreement at all the Shows. Without limiting the generality of Promoter's right to schedule Shows throughout the Term or Artistco's obligation to supply a first class performance of Artist at all such Shows, in no event shall the number of Shows performed by Artist in the first leg of the Tour be less than eighteen (18) Shows unless otherwise directed by Promoter. It shall be unreasonable for Artistco to withhold its approval of adding Shows to any given leg of the Tour or adding legs of Shows to the Tour during the Term (so long as the number of Shows in any given leg do not exceed one per day, and 3.5 per seven-day period, on average) if Promoter demonstrates to Artistco that such additional Shows and/or legs are necessary for Promoter to recoup the Advances in accordance with the terms of this Agreement. Prior to the commencement of any leg of the Tour, Promoter shall provide Artistco with financial models based on estimated Pool Expenses, Production Costs and Pool Revenue based on projections that assume Promoter shall sell tickets to 80% of the sellable capacity of the applicable venues. The parties shall attempt in good faith to agree upon the number of Shows that need to be scheduled for Promoter to recoup all Advances in connection with such leg. As used herein, "leg" refers to a segment of Shows which are contiguous with each other in terms of time and geographic region (e.g., North America, the United Kingdom, Europe) and are not separated by more than three (3) weeks.

4.   **Artist's Compensation.**

4.1   Contingent Compensation. Artist shall be entitled to receive ninety percent (90%) of the Net Pool Revenue, on a fully cross-collateralized basis ("Contingent Compensation"). The Shows and all Pool Revenue and Pool Expenses shall be fully cross-collateralized. A portion of the Contingent Compensation shall be paid to Artistco at the conclusion of each leg of the Tour. Specifically, by no later than ten (10) business days after the final Show in a leg, Promoter shall prepare and deliver to Artist a preliminary settlement of the Shows in such leg within ten (10) business days after the final Show in such leg. Within five (5) business days thereafter, and subject to Promoter's right to recoup Advances, Promoter shall pay Artistco an amount equivalent to ninety percent (90%) of the Contingent Compensation, if any, based on the applicable preliminary settlement. By no later than sixty (60) days after the final Show in the Term, Promoter shall prepare and deliver to Artistco a final settlement of all Pool Revenue and Pool Expenses, on a fully cross-collateralized basis. Within five (5) business days thereafter, Promoter shall pay Artistco any remaining Contingent Compensation owing. Promoter shall retain all other Net Pool Revenue. Notwithstanding any other provision herein, appropriate adjustments shall be made at each of the preliminary settlements and the final settlement to account for any early distribution or overpayment of any portion of the Contingent Compensation, and Artistco shall promptly return any overpayment of Contingent Compensation in the event Promoter determines Artistco was overpaid any portion of the Contingent Compensation. Promoter shall be entitled to offset from amounts owing to Artistco hereunder, any amounts owed by Artistco to Promoter under this Agreement or by reason of any Advances made by Promoter to Artistco throughout the Term. Promoter shall provide Artistco with a bi-weekly accounting of Pool Revenue and Pool Expenses during any leg of the Tour.

4.2   Advances of Contingent Compensation.

4.2.1   Initial Artist Advance.   Conditioned upon the execution and delivery of the inducement letter attached hereto as Exhibit B, the promissory note attached hereto as Exhibit C (which promissory note shall not be secured by any property belonging to Artist, but shall be secured by property owned by Artistco), by Artistco and Artist, Promoter shall loan Artist and Artistco the sum of Five Million United States Dollars (US $5,000,000) (the "Initial Artist Advance") as an advance against Artistco's future entitlement to Contingent Compensation.   Such payment shall be made within four (4) business days of the satisfaction of the foregoing conditions by wire transferring (a) Three Million United States Dollars (US $3,000,000) pursuant to written wiring instructions provided by 2 Seas Records LLC as a payment made on behalf of Artist and/or his affiliate(s) in connection with Artist's settlement with 2 Seas Records LLC; and (b) Two Million United States Dollars (US $2,000,000) to Artistco pursuant to written wiring instructions provided by Artistco.

4.2.2   Advances to Cover Home Rental.   Conditioned upon the execution and delivery of the inducement letter attached hereto as Exhibit B and the promissory note attached hereto as Exhibit C, Promoter shall pay the monthly rent on Artist's home located in Bel Air, California for a period of twelve (12) months at the rate of $100,000 per month (totaling not more than US $1,200,000)) as an additional advance ("Home Rental Advances") against Artistco's future entitlement to Contingent Compensation.   Upon receipt of evidence that Artistco or any member of Artistco's management has paid any such amounts, Promoter shall reimburse such amounts to the applicable person or entity, and such reimbursement (hereinafter, the "Rental Reimbursement") shall be considered part of the Home Rental Advances. At Artistco's request and with the consent of the applicable landlord, Promoter shall secure its obligation to pay such amounts by delivering a letter of credit in favor of the landlord or its designee, which letter of credit shall be in an amount equivalent to One Million Two Hundred Thousand United States Dollars (US $1,200,000) minus the amount of the Rental Reimbursement. Notwithstanding any other provision herein, upon delivering such letter of credit and paying the Rental Reimbursement, Promoter shall be deemed to have fully satisfied its obligations under this provision and the amount of the Home Rental Advances shall be deemed to be the sum of One Million Two Hundred Thousand Dollars (US $1,200,000) plus Promoter's reasonable costs associated with posting such letter of credit. (Artistco and/or Artist may repay a portion of the Home Rental Advances by obtaining from the landlord or its designee, as applicable, the cancellation of the letter of credit delivered by Promoter, in which case the amount of such repayment shall be equivalent to the principal amount remaining on the letter of credit (i.e., the amount that has not yet been drawn down on).

4.2.3   Letter of Credit/Residence Purchase.

(a)   Letter of Credit.   Conditioned upon the issuance of cancellation insurance in accordance with Paragraph 13.1 below, Promoter shall deliver to Artistco an irrevocable standby letter of credit in favor of Artistco in the amount of Fifteen Million United States Dollars (US $15,000,000) in the form substantially similar to the form attached hereto as Exhibit D (the "Letter of Credit"), which Letter of Credit shall require the issuing bank to pay Artistco additional advances against Artistco's future entitlement to Contingent Compensation after every five (5) Shows performed by Artist in an amount equivalent to (a) ninety percent (90%) of the Projected Contingent Compensation for such five (5) Shows minus (b) the sum of the Projected Production Costs allocable to such five (5) Shows and the Artist Advances allocable to such five (5) Shows on a pro rata basis (each, an "Interim Artist

Advance" and collectively, the "Interim Artist Advances"). The amount of the Projected Production Costs and the Artist Advances that shall be allocated to each Show shall be determined by dividing the total amount of the Projected Production Costs by the number of scheduled Shows in the applicable leg and the total amount of the Artist Advances by the number of scheduled Shows in the applicable leg. By no later than three (3) business days after every fifth performances of Shows by Artist, Promoter and Artistco shall execute a written statement ("Joint Statement") verifying that Artist performed at such five (5) Shows and specifying the amount of the Interim Artist Advance, which amount shall be mutually approved at the time the parties agree upon the number of Shows in the applicable leg of the Tour and shall be subject to further modification on an ongoing basis by Promoter based on actual Pool Expenses, Pool Revenue and Production Costs. Thereafter, Artistco shall be entitled to immediately draw down the amount of the Interim Artist Advance from the Letter of Credit. Alternatively, at Promoter's election, in lieu of submitting the Joint Statement to Artistco, Promoter shall be entitled to pay the amount of the Interim Artist Advance directly to Artistco by wire transferring such amount to Artistco by the third business day after the applicable fifth performance by Artist. In the event Promoter pays the Interim Artist Advance to Artistco directly, Artistco and Promoter shall execute an amendment to the Letter of Credit reducing the principal amount of the Letter of Credit by the amount of the Interim Artist Advance paid by Promoter to Artistco.

(b)   Advance to Purchase LV Residence.   In lieu of one or more of the Interim Artist Advances or portions thereof as provided for in Paragraph 4.2.3 (a) above and subject to the below conditions, Artistco may elect to receive a cash advance to assist Artistco or its designee to purchase that certain residence located at ████████████████████████████ (adjacent to the Spanish Trails Golf Course) ("LV Residence") on the following terms:

(i).   The amount of the cash advance (the "LV Residence Advance") shall be the lesser of (a) Fifteen Million United States Dollars (US $15,000,000) minus any Interim Artist Advances previously paid pursuant to Paragraph 4.2.3(a) above, or (b) ninety percent (90%) of the Home Value (defined to be the lesser of (x) the appraised value of the residence based on a written appraisal prepared by a mutually-approved MAI certified appraiser within three (3) months of the purchase of the residence, and (y) the purchase price of such residence).

(ii)   Promoter's obligation to pay such LV Residence Advance shall be conditioned upon (x) the execution and delivery of a mutually-approved promissory note (in a form substantially similar to the promissory note attached hereto as Exhibit C with the principal amount being equivalent to the LV Residence Advance), security agreement and first priority deed of trust by Artistco, Artist and any designee that takes title to the LV Residence, (y) the satisfaction of the conditions set forth in Paragraph 16.4.1 below, and (z) the delivery to Promoter of a lender's title insurance policy in connection with such home purchase in a form approved by Promoter, which demonstrates that Promoter will be the first lienholder on the LV Residence.

(iii)   Artist and Artistco shall purchase and deliver to Promoter a lender's title insurance policy no later than ten (10) business days prior to the closing of the purchase of the LV Residence (the "Closing").

(iv)   Promoter shall pay the LV Residence Advance into the applicable LV Residence escrow by the later of (a) seven (7) business days after all of the conditions set forth in Paragraph 4.2.3(b)(ii) have been satisfied and (b) seven (7) business days before the scheduled Closing;

        (v)   Notwithstanding any other provision herein, in the event the escrow on the LV Residence purchase does not close within ten (10) business days of Promoter's payment of the LV Residence Advance into escrow or any later date approved by Promoter, Artistco shall arrange for escrow to return the LV Residence Advance to Promoter, the LV Residence Advance loan shall be cancelled, and Promoter shall have no further obligation to pay the LV Residence Advance. For the avoidance of doubt, 100% of the LV Residence Advance shall be used by Artist and/or Artistco (or a mutually approved designee) to purchase the LV Residence; and Promoter shall be entitled to receive a recorded first priority lien against the LV Residence for the entire amount of the LV Residence Advance.

        (vi)   In the event Promoter pays the LV Residence Advance (and it is not returned to Promoter in accordance with Paragraph 4.2.3(iv) above, Artistco and Promoter shall execute an amendment to the Letter of Credit reducing the principal amount of the Letter of Credit by the amount of the LV Residence Advance paid by Promoter.

        (vii)   For the avoidance of doubt, Artistco shall be entitled to continue to receive the Interim Artist Advances under Paragraph 4.2.3(a) above until such time as the sum of the Interim Artist Advances paid by Promoter and the LV Residence Advance paid by Promoter, if any, equals Fifteen Million United States Dollars (US $15,000,000) or the Term expires, whichever is earlier.

        4.2.4   <u>Additional Artist Advances</u>. From time to time, upon the execution of a mutually approved promissory note by Artist and Artistco in a form substantially similar to Exhibit C (with appropriate modifications to reflect the actual amount of loan), Promoter may, in its sole discretion, pay Artistco additional advances against Artistco's future entitlement to Contingent Compensation (each; an "Additional Artist Advance," and collectively, "Additional Artist Advances"). (The Initial Artist Advance, the Interim Artist Advances, the LV Residence Advance, the Home Rental Advances and each Additional Artist Advance shall be individually referred to as an "Artist Advance" and collectively referred to as, "Artist Advances").

        4.2.5   <u>Right to Recoup Artist Advances</u>. Promoter shall be entitled to recoup all Artist Advances from Contingent Compensation earned by Artistco or as otherwise agreed by the parties; provided however, Artist and Artistco, on a joint and several basis, shall repay any portion of any such Artist Advances to the extent Promoter does not recoup such Artist Advance within six (6) months after the last scheduled Show in the Tour or such time as Promoter provides written notice to Artist that Promoter does not desire to schedule additional Shows during the Term, whichever is later. Notwithstanding any other provision herein, if by March 1, 2009 (a) Artistco does not obtain cancellation insurance in a form and at a cost approved by Promoter in accordance with Paragraph 13 below, or (b) Promoter is not named as a loss payee on cancellation insurance obtained by Artistco and approved by Promoter in accordance with Paragraph 13 below, or (c) Promoter is unable to obtain cancellation insurance at a reasonable cost to cover its risk of loss of Pool Expenses notwithstanding its good faith efforts to do so, then upon Promoter's written request, which it may make in its sole discretion, Artistco and Artist shall, on a joint and several basis, repay to Promoter any and all Advances by no later than six (6) months after such written request.

5. **Promoter's Responsibilities:** In addition to its other obligations in this Agreement, Promoter shall be responsible for the following during the Term:

5.1 Submission of Proposed Itineraries. From time to time, Promoter shall submit to Artistco proposed itineraries for each leg of a worldwide tour consisting of dates, venues and locations for Shows in particular regions of the Territory. (Any mutually-approved itinerary of Shows shall be referred to as "Approved Itineraries.");

5.2 Book and Promote Shows. Promoter shall use reasonable efforts to book Shows in accordance with Approved Itineraries, and thereafter, Promoter shall place on sale and otherwise actively promote such Shows in a first class manner (and fulfill such other standard promoter obligations for artists of similar caliber to Artist including the arrangement, administration and funding of each item described as an approved "Show Costs"). Promoter shall initiate, negotiate and execute all venue deals;

5.3 Merchandise. Promoter shall use commercially reasonable efforts to enter into an agreement with a mutually-approved merchandising company to manufacture and sell Artist-Merchandise during the Term at Shows and through Artist's official websites;

5.4 Broadcast Opportunities. Promoter shall cooperate with Artist in any broadcast and/or recordation opportunities in connection with one or more Shows on mutually agreeable terms;

5.5 Website Development. Promoter will use reasonable efforts to develop and oversee the administration of an Artist website in accordance with mutually-approved parameters;

5.6 Maximize Net Pool Revenue. Promoter shall use commercially reasonable efforts to maximize Net Pool Revenue and to minimize Production Costs throughout the Term; and

5.7 Sponsorship Agreements. Promoter shall reasonably cooperate with Artistco and Artist to avoid potential conflicts in their respective solicitation of potential mutually approved sponsors, and to conclude Sponsorship Agreements on mutually-approved terms.

6. **Artist Responsibilities.** In addition to their other obligations in this Agreement, Artistco and Artist shall be responsible for the following during the Term:

6.1 Approval of Proposed Itineraries. Artistco shall respond to any itineraries or amended itineraries proposed by Promoter within five (5) business days of receiving the same;

6.2 Performance. A first class performance by Artist at each Show on each of the Approved Itineraries. Artist shall perform no less than 80 minutes at each Show, and the maximum show length (including intermissions and support) for each Show shall be 3.5 hours, pending local curfew restrictions. Artistco and Artist shall approve a sufficient number of Shows on itineraries proposed by Promoter to maximize Promoter's ability to recoup the full amount of the Advances;

6.3 Publicity. Artist to participate in press events at mutually agreed dates and times to launch each leg of the worldwide tour, as well as other mutually-approved publicity, and to participate in the creation of an electronic press kit;

Page | 192

6.4 Broadcast/Recording Opportunities. Artist shall reasonably participate in all mutually-approved broadcast and recordation opportunities related to any Shows;

6.5 Sponsorship Agreements. Artistco shall reasonably cooperate with Promoter to avoid potential conflicts with Promoter's solicitation of potential mutually-approved sponsors and to conclude Sponsorship Agreements on mutually-approved terms. Artist shall reasonably participate in fulfillment requirements of Sponsorship Agreements (e.g., attend meet and greets, permit reasonable sponsorship signage);

6.6 Maximize Net Pool Revenue. Artist and Artistco shall use commercially reasonable efforts to maximize Net Pool Revenue and to minimize Production Costs throughout the Term;

6.7 Inducement Letter. Artist shall execute and deliver the inducement letter attached as Exhibit B;

6.8 Management, Agency and Legal Costs. With the exception of the monthly fee owing under the terms of a separate agreement with TT International, LLC for the services of Dr. Tohme Tohme (not to exceed $100,000 per month), which shall be included in Production Costs, Artistco shall be solely responsible for and shall pay all costs associated with management and agency commissions or fees and legal fees of Artist and/or Artistco, if any;

6.9 Delivery of Pool Revenue to Promoter. Artistco and Artist shall deliver any Pool Revenue received by them to Promoter for disbursement in accordance with this Agreement; and

6.10 Positive Public Image. Throughout the Term, Artist shall use his best efforts to maintain a positive public perception of Artist, and Artist shall not conduct himself in a manner that will negatively impact the reputation of the Artist or Promoter.

7. **Ticketing Activities:**

7.1 Complimentary Tickets. Except as otherwise mutually approved, there shall be no complimentary tickets issued except for ten (10) complimentary tickets for Artistco's use per Show, and complimentary tickets used for promotional purposes and to satisfy venue license agreements and Sponsorship Agreements.

7.2 Ticket and Secondary Ticket Sales. Promoter shall control ticket sales and secondary ticket activities, with inventory for ticket auctions and other secondary ticket programs in a first hold position.

8. **Production of the Shows.**

8.1 Production Services. Promoter shall provide producer services in connection with the design and production of the Show including, without limitation, working closely with the Artist regarding creative aspects of the design of the Show, managing the production in accordance with mutually-approved parameters and a mutually-approved production budget, and engaging the services of third

Page | 193

party vendors to assist in the production of the Show. The parties will work together to prepare a mutually-approved tour rider for the Shows.

8.2   Production Advances. Subject to Paragraph 16.4 below, Promoter shall make advances to cover mutually-approved Production Costs ("Production Advances") up to but not exceeding Seven Million Five Hundred Thousand United States Dollars (US $7,500,000) ("Production Advance Cap") plus the mutually-approved cost of mutually-approved cancellation insurance acquired to cover the risk of loss of Artistco's profits and Production Costs in a collective amount that equals any unrecouped portion of the Advances; provided, however, Promoter shall pay such Production Advances directly to third party vendors upon presentation of proper invoice(s). Promoter shall keep Artistco informed of such Production Advances.   Promoter shall be entitled to recoup such Production Advances from Contingent Compensation otherwise payable to Artistco. By no later than ten (10) business days after the end of the Term, Artistco shall repay Promoter any portion of such Production Advance to the extent Promoter does not recoup such Production Advances from Artistco's Contingent Compensation.   Artistco shall be responsible for all Production Costs requested by Artistco in excess of the Production Advance Cap ("Excess Production Costs"), and Artistco shall reimburse to Promoter or otherwise advance all funds necessary to pay such Excess Production Costs. Artistco shall be responsible for all of Artist's management and/or agency commissions or fees, all legal fees incurred by or at the request of Artistco and/or Artist in connection with this Agreement or the Shows and all production related costs incurred by or at the request of Artistco and/or Artist which are not included in the definition of Production Costs.

8.3   Producer's Fee. Artistco shall pay Promoter a producer's fee ("Producer's Fee") in an amount equal to five percent (5%) of the Artist's Net Tour Income. Promoter shall be entitled to deduct the Producer's Fee from amounts payable to Artistco hereunder.

9.   **Broadcasting and Recordation Opportunities.** Subject to the rights of Artist's label and publishers, if any, the parties shall reasonably cooperate with each other in broadcast and recordation opportunities in connection with Artist's performance(s) at one or more Shows, Artist shall own the same, and the parties shall jointly exploit the same and all derivations therefrom in perpetuity in all modes of distribution or transmission, now known or hereinafter discovered (e.g., DVD, television, cable, satellite, cellular, IPTV, webcasting, Internet). Net Show-Related Broadcast/Recording Revenue received during the Term shall be included in Pool Revenue. Net Show-Related Broadcast/Recording Revenue received after the Term shall be paid first to Promoter to the extent it has not recouped Advances, mutually-approved costs associated with Net Show-Related Broadcast/Recording Revenue and the production of the underlying intellectual property right, and Pool Expenses, and thereafter, such amounts shall be disbursed ninety percent (90%) to Artistco and ten percent (10%) to Promoter. Notwithstanding any other provision in this Agreement, the parties' rights and obligations associated with Net Show-Related Broadcast/Recording Revenue shall survive the expiration or termination of the Term.

10.   **Accountings / Show Settlement / Audit:**

10.1   Show Settlements: Artistco shall have the right to have a representative participate in all show settlements. Promoter shall provide Artistco with a written settlement for each Show, which shall contain the itemized calculation of Pool Revenue and Pool Expenses for each Show.

10.2   Audit Rights.   Promoter shall keep complete, detailed and accurate books and records of all Pool Revenue, Pool Expenses, Production Costs and Advances during the Term, as well as any Net Show-Related Broadcast/Recording Revenue received after the Term. Artistco shall keep complete, detailed and accurate books and records of all Pool Revenue received by Artistco in respect of the Shows, as well as any Net Show-Related Broadcast/Recording Revenue received after the Term. During the Term and for twenty-four (24) months thereafter, each of the parties shall provide the other party, upon reasonable notice, with full and complete access during regular business hours at such party's normal place of business to such party's Show-related books and records to inspect and copy, and to perform, at the discretion and expense of the other party, audits or reviews of such books and records.

11.   **Approvals.** In addition to any other approval rights set forth herein, Artistco and Promoter shall each have the right to pre-approve before any Show, the following significant business matters relating to such Show: (a) any itinerary changes including any and all decisions to add multiple dates; (b) any travel and/or VIP packages to the extent the same involves any participation by Artist; (c) marketing and promotional activities to the extent the same involved any participation by Artist or the use of Artist's name and/or likeness; (d) the date and location of each performance of Artist under this Agreement, subject to Promoter's rights under Paragraph 3 above; (e) complimentary tickets for each Show; (f) the identity of any sponsors and the terms and conditions of Sponsorship Agreements; and (g) the dates and times of any publicity events at which Artist is required to participate. With the exception of those matters over which a party is expressly given sole discretion under the terms of this Agreement, no party may withhold, delay or condition approval unreasonably with respect to any matter for which such party's approval or consent is required by this Agreement. Notwithstanding Artistco's approval rights, in the event Artistco unreasonably withholds, delays or qualifies Artistco's approval over any such matter, Artistco shall be deemed to have given its approval over such matter.

12.   **Force Majeure.** If a Force Majeure Event prevents the presentation of one or more Shows in the manner required by or reasonably expected under the terms of this Agreement, then absent a mutual agreement to the contrary, (i) such Show shall be canceled, (ii) neither party hereto shall be in default of its obligations by reason of such cancellation, (iii) both parties hereto shall use all reasonable efforts to reschedule such Show at a mutually agreeable time and place, and in a manner that avoids disproportionate costs or harm to either party; and (iv) except to the extent a cancelled Show has been rescheduled by the parties to a mutually approved date and location, Artistco shall return any portion of the Artist Advances allocable to such cancelled Show (which shall be determined by dividing the total amount of the Artist Advances by the number of scheduled Shows in the applicable leg), and each party shall be responsible for its own expenses (except for Pool Expenses associated with a cancelled Show, which shall be recoupable from Pool Revenue and Production Expenses incurred by Promoter, which shall be recoupable in accordance with the other terms of this Agreement). No party shall be in default of any obligation under this Agreement if its performance of such obligation is rendered impossible by reason of a Force Majeure Event.

13.   **Insurance.**

13.1   Cancellation Insurance. Artist shall approve and reasonably cooperate in Promoter's acquisition of life insurance, non-performance, cancellation and other insurance, subject to reasonable confidentiality restrictions. Upon Promoter's request, Artist shall be required to undertake physical examination(s) by an independent physician and shall provide related health and medical information as reasonably requested by Promoter's insurers and/or such independent physician, with a right to have his own doctor present and to receive copies of any and all medical reports prepared by such independent physician. The applicable insurance companies and physicians must agree to hold such medical reports in the strictest confidence. Artistco hereby represents and warrants that Artist does not possess any known health conditions, injuries or ailments that would reasonably be expected to interfere with Artist's first class performance at each of the Shows during the Term. In addition, Artistco shall acquire cancellation insurance, if available and mutually-approved, to cover the risk of loss of Artistco's profits and Production Costs in an amount that, at a minimum, will equal or exceed any unrecouped portion of the Advances, and Artistco shall name Promoter as a loss payee thereon. As a loss payee, Promoter shall be entitled to receive insurance proceeds directly as a means of recouping any unrecouped portion of the Advances; provided that such right shall not in any way relieve Artistco of any of its obligations to repay Advances to Promoter. To the extent Promoter has already recouped such Advances, Promoter shall deliver any insurance proceeds Promoter receives as a loss payee under Artistco's cancellation insurance policy directly to Artistco. The cost of such cancellation insurance shall be included in Production Costs to the extent it is mutually-approved. Promoter may, in its sole discretion, obtain cancellation insurance to cover the risk of loss of Pool Expenses and/or Promoter's profits hereunder. In the event Promoter purchases cancellation insurance to cover the risk of loss of Pool Expenses, the cost of such insurance shall be a Pool Expense.

13.2   Liability Insurance. Each party shall obtain CGL (with limits of no less than US $10,000,000 per occurrence and in the aggregate); automobile and worker's compensation insurance on terms required by Promoter, and shall name the other party and any person or entity reasonably designated by the other party on the foregoing CGL and automobile policies, with such endorsements reasonably requested by Promoter.

14.   **Termination**. Either party shall be entitled to terminate this Agreement if the other party fails to substantially perform its material obligations hereunder, and such failure to perform is not covered by a Force Majeure Event (the "Defaulting Party"), in a manner that results in material harm, loss or other damage to the other party ("Event of Default"), and if curable, such Event of Default is not cured within ten (10) business days after receipt by the Defaulting Party of written notice thereof, or in the event such Event of Default is curable but is not reasonably capable of being cured within such period, and the Defaulting Party either fails to begin the cure within such period or fails to diligently pursues such cure to completion as promptly as possible. Artist and Artistco's obligations to return the Advances shall survive any termination of this Agreement.

15.   **Indemnification**.

15.1   Promoter shall defend, indemnify and hold Artistco and Artist, and their respective affiliates, employees, agents and representatives (the "Artist-Related Indemnitees") harmless from any Third Party Claims arising out of or related to (a) Promoter's breach of any of Promoter's obligations, representations and/or warranties under this Agreement; and (b) the negligence, and/or wrongful acts or omissions (including in the infringement of the intellectual property rights of third parties) of Promoter, if any, in connection with the presentation of a Show(s); provided however, in no event shall Promoter be responsible for any Claims arising out of or related to either (x) the negligence or willful misconduct of any such Artist-Related Indemnitees, or (b) Artistco's breach of any of Artistco's obligations under this Agreement.

Page | 196

15.2   Artistco and Artist shall defend, indemnify and hold Promoter and its respective affiliates, employees, agents and representatives (the "Promoter-Related Indemnitees") harmless from any Third Party Claims arising out of or related to (a) Artistco's breach of any of Artistco's obligations, representations and/or warranties under this Agreement; (b) the Artist's use of Pyrotechnics, if any; (c) the staging, props, stunts, Artist movements and other production elements associated with the Show; and (d) the negligence or wrongful acts or omissions (including in the infringement of the intellectual property rights of third parties) of Artistco, Artist and/or the Tour Party, if any, in connection with a Show(s); provided however, in no event shall Artistco be responsible for any Claims arising out of or related to (x) the negligence or willful misconduct of any such Promoter-Related Indemnitees, or (y) Promoter's breach of any of Promoter's obligations under this Agreement.

16.   **Miscellaneous**.

16.1   Integrated Agreement. This Agreement, with its Exhibits, is intended by the parties to be the complete and final expression of their agreement, and is specifically intended to be an integrated contract with respect to the matters affected herein. Each party agrees that any prior negotiations, statements, representations or agreements with respect to the subject matter herein are merged in and superseded by this Agreement, and that such party has not relied on any representation or promise, oral or otherwise, which is not set forth in this Agreement. This Agreement may not be modified or amended except by a writing signed by the party to be bound.

16.2   Confidentiality. All of the material supplied to each of the parties by the other which is of a confidential nature shall be the sole and exclusive property of the party producing such material, and each of the parties shall keep the material confidential and refrain from disclosing such material to any third party (except for the parties' respective representatives who agree to honor such confidentiality) without the express written consent of the other party. The material terms of this Agreement shall be kept confidential except to the extent necessary to enforce the terms hereof or as required to comply with the law (such as for example, pursuant to a court order, or where a party must disclose such information to a tax advisor or accountant for purposes of preparing tax returns or financial statements).

16.3   Security. To secure the faithful performance of Artistco of Artistco's and Artist's obligations under this Agreement (including to repay the Advances), Artistco hereby grants Promoter a lien in all of Artistco's right, title and interest in, to, and under the following properties, assets and rights, wherever located, whether now owned or hereafter acquired or arising, and all proceeds and products thereof (all of the same being hereinafter referred to collectively as, the "Collateral"): contract rights or rights to the payment of money in which Artistco and/or Artist has an interest, insurance claims and proceeds, commercial tort claims, securities and all other investment property, and all general intangibles (including all accounts receivable and payment intangibles). Artistco shall reasonably cooperate with Promoter in its efforts to perfect such security interest.

16.4   Conditions to Advances.

16.4.1 Notwithstanding any other provision of this Agreement, except to the extent waived by Promoter, with the exception of the Initial Artist Advance, Promoter shall have no obligation to pay any Advances until such time as (a) cancellation insurance in a mutually-approved form is issued in favor of Artistco to cover its risk of loss of profits and Production Costs sufficient to cover all unrecouped Advances, and (b) Artistco delivers to Promoter evidence satisfactory to Promoter that Promoter has been named as a loss payee under such cancellation insurance obtained by Artistco in a form approved by Promoter, and (c) Artistco delivers to Promoter evidence satisfactory to Promoter that the dispute with 2 Seas Records LLC has been settled and Artistco abides by all terms and conditions of such settlement, and (d) Artistco and Promoter have approved in writing particulars of the applicable leg of the Tour that pertain to such Advances (e.g., tour itinerary, public on-sale dates; ticket prices and scaling; secondary ticket activities, approval over budgets for Production Costs and Pool Expenses, Projected Contingent Compensation, and Projected Production Costs); and (e) cancellation insurance in a form approved by Promoter is issued in favor of Promoter to cover its risk of loss of Pool Expenses.

16.4.2 Notwithstanding any other provision of this Agreement, except to the extent waived by Promoter, Promoter shall have no obligation to pay the Initial Advance until such time as Artistco delivers to Promoter evidence satisfactory to Promoter that the dispute with 2 Seas Records LLC has been settled and that Artistco has either paid the amounts owing to 2 Seas Records LLC under such settlement agreement or will pay such amounts (including by permitting some or all of the Initial Advance to be paid to 2 Seas Records LLC). For the avoidance of doubt, Promoter shall be entitled, in its sole discretion, to waive or refuse to waive any of the conditions precedent to its obligation to pay any of the Advances.

16.5 . <u>Agreement Not Assignable</u>. Except as otherwise provided in this Agreement, no party hereto may assign its rights or obligations under this Agreement to any other person or entity without the prior written consent of the other party; provided, however, Promoter shall be entitled to assign its rights and obligations under this Agreement to an affiliate for purposes of promoting Shows outside the United States, if any, provided that Promoter shall remain principally responsible for all of its obligations.

16.6 <u>Severable</u>. If any provision of this Agreement or the application thereof is held invalid, the invalidity shall not affect other provisions or applications of this Agreement; provided that the material terms of this Agreement can be given their intended effect without the invalid provisions, and to this extent the provisions of this Agreement are declared to be severable.

16.7 <u>Governing Law/Forum</u>. This Agreement, and the parties' conduct arising out of or related to it, shall be governed by California law, without regard to its choice of law rules. Any dispute arising out of or related to this Agreement must be brought in federal or state court in Los Angeles County, and the parties hereby consent to the exclusive jurisdiction and venue of such forum.

16.8 <u>Notices</u>. All notices, approvals, and consents required or permitted to be given hereunder, or which are given with respect to this Agreement, shall be in writing, and shall be deemed duly given or made (i) upon delivery or refusal of such delivery of such notice by a recognized courier service (which shall be deemed to be given upon delivery if delivered on a business day, or the next business day if delivered on a holiday or weekend); (ii) upon personal delivery (which shall be deemed to have been given upon delivery) (which shall be deemed to be given upon delivery if delivered on a business day, or the next business day if delivered on a holiday or weekend); or (iii) upon delivery by fax machine capable of confirming receipt (which shall be deemed to be given upon delivery if delivered on a business day, or the next business day if delivered on a holiday or weekend), and in each case addressed as follows (or at such other address for a party as shall be specified in a notice so given):

To Artistco
and Artist: The Michael Jackson Company, LLC

███████████████████████████████
███████████████████████

Attn: Dr. Tohme Tohme

███████████████████
███████████████████

With a simultaneous copy to:

Dr. Tohme Tohme

██████████████████████████████
████████████████████
████████████████████
█████████████████

Dennis J. Hawk, Esq.

██████████████████████
███████████████████████
███████████████████
██████████████

To Promoter: AEG Live, LLC

████████████████████████
███████████████████████

Attn: General Counsel

███████████████████
███████████████████

With a simultaneous copy to:

Luce Forward Hamilton & Scripps LLP

███████████████████
████████████████

Attn: Kathy A. Jorrie

████████████████████
████████████████

16.9   Counterpart/Fax Signatures. This Agreement may be executed in any number of counterparts, each of which shall be deemed an original, and facsimile copies or photocopies of signatures shall be as valid as originals.

By signing below each party acknowledges its agreement to the foregoing and agrees to negotiate the definitive agreement expeditiously and in good faith.

Very truly yours,

AEG LIVE, LLC

Brandon K. Phillips
President & CEO
AEG Live LLC

We have read the above, and agree to the terms.

THE MICHAEL JACKSON COMPANY, LLC   MICHAEL JACKSON

Name: Michael Jackson   Michael Jackson

Exhibit A

Definitions

1.   "**Advances**" refers to Artist Advances and Production Advances.

2.   "**Artist Merchandise**" means any merchandise bearing the name, likeness or logos of Artist.

3.   "**Artist's Net Tour Income**" means the Contingent Compensation minus the sum of Production Costs plus the portion of the Contingent Compensation that consists of Merchandise Revenue (defined below), Net Show-Related Broadcast/Recording Revenue (defined below) and Net Fan Club Membership Revenue (defined below).

4.   "**Force Majeure Event**" means the occurrence of an event outside the reasonable control of the party claiming the benefit of the force majeure event, such as an illness or accident to the Artist (which, in those situations where Artistco is the party seeking the protection of such occurrence only, could not be avoided by Artist through reasonable diligence), other accident, an act or regulation of public authority, fire, riot or civil commotion, lockout or strike or other labor dispute, terrorist acts, acts or declarations of war; disease, death, epidemic, substantial interruption in, or substantial delay or failure of, technical facilities, failure or substantial and extraordinary delay of necessary transportation services, war conditions, emergencies, acts of God, or any other similar or dissimilar occurrence beyond the reasonable control of the party claiming the benefit of the Force Majeure provision. In the event of a strike or labor dispute of the musician union, any reasonable fee or penalty imposed on Artistco or Artist as the result of the Artist crossing a picket line will be a Pool Expense. Notwithstanding the foregoing, poor weather conditions shall not constitute a "Force Majeure Event" unless such conditions prevent the attendance by or adversely affect the safety of the Artist, the public attending or desiring to attend the applicable Shows or persons reasonably necessary to carry out the performance of the Artist at a Show.

5.   "**Net Pool Revenue**" means Pool Revenue generated during the Term less Pool Expenses incurred during the Term, on a fully cross-collateralized basis.

6.   "**Pool Revenue**" means the aggregate of the following:

        a.   "**Adjusted Gross Ticket Revenue**" (defined to be gross ticket proceeds received by Promoter, Artistco and/or Artist from Shows less taxes, facility fees, restoration charges and credit card commissions);

        b.   Show specific ticket rebates, expense savings, refunds or rebates, if any, received by Promoter, Artistco or Artist from whatever source (e.g., Ticketmaster, VIP and fan club tickets) in connection with any and all Shows;

        c.   Sponsorship revenue related to sponsorship of any Show from whatever source and in whatever nature received by Promoter, Artistco or Artist (or any respective affiliate) including, without limitation, in connection with any Sponsorship Agreement. In-kind sponsorship consideration (e.g., marketing or media exposure, etc.) shall be treated as a cash equivalent and deemed Pool Revenue;

Page | 201

d. Interest income, if any, received by tour;

e. Sell-off proceeds from third party promoters in connection with any Show, in which event, no Pool Expenses associated with such sold-off Show shall be included in Pool Expenses hereunder unless such Pool Expenses have been paid directly by Promoter and Promoter is not reimbursed by the applicable sell-off promoter;

f. Revenue received by Promoter, Artist or Artistco from ticket auctions, Ticket Exchange and other secondary ticket activities and ancillary ticketing activities (including, without limitation, VIP packages, travel packages, fan club tickets, corporate packages, dinner packages, Ticketmaster auctions, promotional party packages, American Express ticket programs (e.g., "Early on Sale" program), should Promoter make arrangements for the same), in connection with any and all Shows;

g. "Merchandise Revenue" (defined to be any and all revenue received by Promoter, Artist and/or Artistco under any such parties' agreement a mutually-approved merchandise company from the sale of Artist Merchandise at the venue of each Show and through Artist's Official website during the Term;

h. "Net Show-Related Broadcast/Recording Revenue" (defined to be Show-related broadcast and/or recording revenue generated from the live and/or delayed broadcast (in any and all modes of transmission (e.g., television, webcasts, cellular, IPTV, cable, satellite) or recordation of any portion of Artist's performance at any Show, and all derivative products associated therewith to the extent the same exceeds actual costs incurred by Artistco/Artist to generate such revenue);

i. "Net Fan Club Membership Revenue" (defined to be any and all revenue received by Artist and/or Artistco (with an understanding that such parties will receive such revenue) during the Term from membership fees or other fees payable by Fan Club Members or any other form of memberships ("Fan Club Memberships") or fees payable to echo or such other mutually-approved website design vendor to the extent the same exceeds actual costs incurred by Artistco/Artist associated with such matters; and

j. Any other revenue received by Promoter, Artistco or Artist in connection with the Shows.

7. "Pool Expenses" means the following:

a. Customary and mutually-approved show costs incurred by Promoter in connection with any and all Shows (e.g., venue rentals, net advertising, marketing material, public liability insurance, security, ticketing costs, local staff, venue staff, power, venue expenses related to pre-rigs, roof rental relating to outdoor shows); provided however, for the avoidance of doubt, shows costs from Shows sold off by Promoter to third parties shall not be included in Pool Expenses and shall not be cross-collateralized with Shows promoted by Promoter;

b. The cost of mutually-approved support talent, if any, at any Shows;

c.   Mutually agreeable expenses associated with secondary ticketing activities and ancillary ticketing activities in connection with Shows;

d.   Cancellation insurance covering the risk of loss of Pool Expenses (inclusive of mutually-approved advertising, venue rent and other direct show costs) on Shows throughout the Territory, if any, provided that the cancellation insurance shall be placed through customary channels;

e.   Mutually agreeable expenses required by mutually-approved tour rider in connection with any and all Shows;

f.   Mutually-approved costs incurred by Promoter in connection with the manufacture and sale of Artist Merchandise;

g.   Ad mat and advertising materials (e.g., radio spot, print ads, television, etc.) associated with the Shows;

h.   Sponsorship commissions (including commissions owing to either party's affiliates) and related fulfillment expenses;

i.   3rd party ticket sales commissions and related expenses; and

j.   Other customary documented mutually-approved tour pool expenses.

8.   **"Production Costs"** means the following costs to the extent they relate to Shows and are mutually-approved: (a) all Artist-related production and related costs including, but not limited to, sound and lights, rigging motors, staging elements, video (if any), pyro (if any), photos and bios of Artist, televised broadcasts, if any; (b) the cost of all musical instruments of the tour party and the cost of transporting, storing and insuring all such musical instruments; (c) personnel costs for the tour party (including transportation, food and accommodations); (d) salaries, wages, per diems, payroll taxes and expenses, union dues and other labor costs and benefits of musicians and dancers and other non-management members of the Tour Party; (e) at such time as Artistco obtains the cancellation insurance required by Paragraph 13 of the Agreement and Promoter receives written evidence that it has been named as a loss payee of such cancellation insurance, the mutually approved direct, actual costs of Artist-related management and staffing pursuant to the terms of a separate agreement with TT International, LLC for the services of Dr. Tohme Tohme (not to exceed $100,000 per month); (e) travel and transportation costs (including trucking, bussing and freight, and local ground and show transportation for the tour party; (f) tour design fees and tour creative art; (g) visa & immigration costs, if any, for the tour party; (h) all such other costs for which an artist (or its furnishing company) is customarily responsible, including, without limitation, adequate worker's compensation and liability and other insurance with respect to the foregoing; provided however, in no event shall Production Costs include any other costs associated with management and agency commissions or fees and legal fees of Artist and/or Artistco, all of which shall remain the sole responsibility of Artistco and Artist); and (i) cancellation insurance, if available and mutually-approved, to cover the risk of loss of Artistco's profits and Production Costs in an amount which, at a minimum, is equivalent to or exceeds any unrecouped portion of the Advances and costs related to naming Promoter as a loss payee on such insurance.

9.   "**Projected Contingent Compensation**" shall mean the amount of the Contingent Compensation per Show projected by Promoter based on the projected Pool Revenues and Pool Expenses for the mutually agreed number of Shows in the applicable leg of the Tour based on an assumption that Promoter will sell tickets to 80% of the sellable capacity of the applicable Shows. Promoter may adjust the amount of the Projected Contingent Compensation on an ongoing basis based on the addition of Shows to the applicable leg of the Tour, actual Pool Revenues and actual Pool Expenses.

10.   "**Projected Production Costs**" shall mean the Production Costs projected by Promoter on a per Show basis based on the mutually agreed number of Shows at the venues set forth on the mutually approved itinerary in the applicable leg of the Tour. Promoter may adjust the Projected Production Costs on an ongoing basis based on the addition of Shows to the applicable leg of the Tour and actual Production Costs.

11.   "**Shows**" means any and all mutually-approved shows to be performed by Artist (each, a "Show" and collectively, the "Shows") during the Term throughout the Territory.

12.   "**Sponsorship Agreements**" refers to any mutually-approved agreement wherein a third party receives sponsorship or comparable credit or publicity customary for sponsors in Show-related advertisements, signage or other things.

13.   "**Territory**" means the world.

14.   "**Term**" means the execution date through December 31, 2011, or the conclusion of a Worldwide touring cycle which includes Shows throughout the major touring territories of the World as mutually selected by Artistco and Promoter, whichever occurs later ("Expiration Date"); provided however, Promoter shall have the right in its sole discretion, but not the obligation, to (a) extend the Term beyond the Expiration Date by written notice(s) until such time as Promoter recoups one hundred percent (100%) of the Advances; or (b) end the Term prior to the Expiration Date, in which event the Term shall be defined to end on the date(s) selected by Promoter, notwithstanding the Expiration Date. To exercise its right to extend the term under the foregoing provision, Promoter must give written notice of its desire to extend the term prior to December 31, 2011. For the avoidance of doubt, Artistco and Promoter shall have all of their respective rights and obligations under this Agreement with respect to any mutually approved Shows that have been scheduled prior to the Expiration Date and are to be performed after the Expiration Date as the result of Promoter's decision to extend the Term regardless of whether or not Promoter recoups one hundred percent of the Advances prior to the completion of such Shows. Notwithstanding any of the foregoing, in the event the Term is extended by the provisions of this paragraph beyond December 31, 2011, Artistco shall have the right to end the Term on the New Expiration Date (defined below) by giving Promoter written notice by facsimile transmission (the "Buy-Out Notice") of Artistco's desire to end the Term on the New Expiration Date, which Buy-Out Notice may be given on December 31, 2011, or any date thereafter, and upon receipt of such Buy-Out Notice, the Term shall then end on the later of (a) the date of Promoter's receipt of the Buy-Out Notice, or (b) the completion of any mutually-approved Shows previously scheduled (such later date being referred to as the "New Expiration Date"), but only so long as Artistco pays to Promoter an amount equivalent to any unrecouped portion of the Advances as of such New Expiration Date by no later than ten (10) business days after Promoter delivers the final settlement of the Tour.

15. **"Third Party Claims"** refers to claim(s), losses, liabilities, judgments, suits, actions, damages and expenses (including reasonable attorney's fees and expenses of counsel of the indemnified party).

Exhibit 1

Joint Confirmation

Bank
Bank Address
Attn: _____
Telephone: (___) _____
Facsimile: (___) _____

Re: AEG Live/The Michael Jackson Company, LLC– Michael Jackson ("Artist") (with respect to [dates] Shows at [**venue, city**], and Draw Number [____])

Dear Sir or Madame:

In accordance with that certain Tour Agreement by and between AEG Live LLC ("Promoter") and The Michael Jackson Company, LLC("Artistco"), we hereby confirm that Artist has performed at the above reference five Shows and that the Interim Artist Advance that is now owing by Promoter to Artistco is $_____ ("Interim Artist Advance").

AEG LIVE LLC

By: _____

Print Name of Authorized Signer: _____

Dated: _____

THE MICHAEL JACKSON COMPANY, LLC.

By: _____

Print Name of Authorized Signer: _____

Dated: _____

Please be aware that we are hereby drawing under the above referenced Letter of Credit and that:

1) Applicant owes us as of the date hereof the Interim Artist Advance in the amount specified on the attached Exhibit 1 (Joint Letter signed by authorized representatives of Applicant and Beneficiary) in connection with Applicant's obligations to make certain advances (known as "Interim Artist Advances") to Beneficiary under the terms of the Tour Agreement dated January 26, 2009 made between Applicant, Beneficiary and Michael Jackson in relation to the worldwide concert tour of Michael Jackson (herein referred to as "the Agreement");

2) We have requested payment from Applicant in the amount of [*Amount of Interim Artist Advance*] and as of the date hereof Applicant has declined to pay us for such amount, instead opting for us to drawn down on this Letter of Credit in such amount.

3) This drawing is in the amount of [*Amount of Interim Artist Advance*], which is not in excess of the amount owing and for which payment has been requested as set forth in paragraphs (1) and (2) hereof.

4) We hereby instruct you to wire [*Amount of Interim Artist Advance*] to Beneficiary pursuant to the following wiring instructions:

> [BANK NAME]
> [BANK ADDRESS]
> ABA Routing No.
> Account No.
> Reference: AEG Live LLC/Michael Jackson

....
(authorized signatory 1)
The Michael Jackson Company, LLC

....
(authorized signatory 2)
The Michael Jackson Company, LLC"

Partial and multiple drawings are permitted. The stated amount of this letter of credit shall be automatically reduced by the amount of any drawings honored by us hereunder.

SPECIAL CONDITIONS: -- [As reasonably required by the Issuing Bank].

AUTHORIZED SIGNATURE _____

Exhibit D

Standby Letter of Credit

[BANK LETTERHEAD]

LETTER OF CREDIT NUMBER	:	_____
DATE OF ISSUE	:	_____, 2009
EXPIRY DATE	:	December 31, 2009
PLACE OF PRESENTATION OF	:	_____
CURRENCY/AMOUNT	:	USD $15,000,000 (FIFTEEN MILLION U.S. DOLLARS AND 00/100)
APPLICANT	:	AEG LIVE, LLC
		████████████████
		████████████████

BENEFICIARY	:	The Michael Jackson Company, LLC
		████████████████
		████████████████

Attention: Dr. Tohme Tohme

We hereby establish an irrevocable standby letter of credit in favor of The Michael Jackson Company, LLC (herein called "Beneficiary") for the account of AEG Live LLC (herein called "Applicant") which is available by payment of Beneficiary's draft at sight drawn on us pursuant to the wire transfer instructions set forth in paragraph 4 of the below-referenced Drawing Certification) bearing the clause "drawn under [bank's] letter of credit no. _____ dated _____ and accompanied by this original letter of credit, any amendment(s) hereto (if any), a written verification signed by Brandon K. Phillips, John Meglen, Rick Webking or Shawn Trell on behalf of Applicant or such other person designated by any such individual in writing, and by Dr. Tohme Tohme on behalf of Beneficiary or such other person designated by Dr. Tohme Tohme or Michael Jackson of Beneficiary in writing attesting to the performance of Michael Jackson ("Artist") at five separate shows in the form attached hereto as Exhibit 1 and specifying the amount of the Interim Artist Advance that is owing by Beneficiary; and a written drawing certification in the form as follows:

"Drawing Certification
to [*NAME & FULL ADDRESS OF BANK*]

Re: Irrevocable Letter of Credit No. [*number*]

Page | 208

To Maker: The Michael Jackson Company, LLC
Michael Jackson

███████████████████████

Attn: Dr. Tohme Tohme and Michael Jackson

███████████████████
███████████████

With a copy to:

Business Law Group

███████████████████
███████████████

Attn: Dennis Hawk

███████████████████
███████████████

To Holder: AEG Live, LLC

████████████████████████

Attn: General Counsel

███████████████████
███████████████

GOVERNING LAW

This Note shall be governed by and construed under the laws of the State of California. This Note shall be deemed made, entered into and delivered in Los Angeles County, California, and the Maker hereof hereby submits and consents to the exclusive jurisdiction and venue in the Superior Court of California for the County of Los Angeles.

THE MICHAEL JACKSON COMPANY, LLC

By: _____
Michael Jackson
An authorized representative

MICHAEL JACKSON

By: _____
Michael Jackson
An Individual

MAXIMUM INTEREST

In no event whatsoever shall the amount paid, or agreed to be paid, to Holder for the use, forbearance or detention of money to be loaned hereunder or otherwise, for the performance or payment of any covenant or obligation contained herein, exceed the maximum amount permissible under applicable law; If from any circumstance whatsoever fulfillment of any provision hereof exceeds the limit of validity prescribed by law, then, ipso facto, the obligation to be fulfilled shall be reduced to the limit of such validity, and if from any such circumstance Holder shall ever receive as interest under this Note or otherwise an amount that would exceed the highest lawful rate, such amount that would be excessive interest shall be applied to the reduction of the principal amount owing hereunder and not to the payment of interest, or if such excessive interest exceeds the unpaid balance of principal, such excess shall be refunded to Maker.

PREPAYMENT

Subject to the remaining provisions of this paragraph, Maker may prepay this Note in full or in part at any time without prepayment charge. No partial prepayment shall release Maker from thereafter tendering all regular scheduled monthly payments required herein until the Note is paid in full. Any and all prepayments shall be applied directly towards principal. Maker shall receive a dollar for dollar reduction of the Note for any prepayments made by Maker or Maker's designee, representative and/or agent.

MISCELLANEOUS

The terms of this Note shall inure to the benefit of and bind the parties hereto and their successors and assigns. As used herein; the term "Maker" shall include the undersigned Maker and any other person or entity who may subsequently become liable for payment hereof. The term "Holder" shall include the named Holder as well as any other person or entity to whom this Note or any interest in this Note is conveyed, transferred or assigned. Each person signing this Note on behalf of Maker represents and warrants that he has full authority to do so and that this Note and Security Agreement binds Maker (i.e., both Artistco and Artist). This Note may not be modified or amended except by a writing signed by each Maker and Holder.

NOTICE

All notices, approvals, and consents required or permitted to be given hereunder, or which are given with respect to this Agreement, shall be in writing, and shall be deemed duly given or made (i) upon delivery or refusal of such delivery of such notice by a recognized courier service (which shall be deemed to be given upon delivery if delivered on a business day, or the next business day if delivered on a holiday or weekend); (ii) upon personal delivery (which shall be deemed to have been given upon delivery) (which shall be deemed to be given upon delivery if delivered on a business day, or the next business day if delivered on a holiday or weekend); or (iii) upon delivery by fax machine capable of confirming receipt (which shall be deemed to be given upon delivery if delivered on a business day, or the next business day if delivered on a holiday or weekend); and in each case addressed as follows (or at such other address for a party as shall be specified in a notice so given):

Page | 210

(i) default shall be made in the payment of any installment hereunder when due, and such default is not cured within five (5) business days after written notice thereof by Holder to Maker;

(ii) default in any other obligation contained herein, which default is not cured within five (5) business days after written notice of such default has been given by Holder to Maker; or

(iii) if Maker shall make a general assignment for the benefit of creditors, or shall file or have filed against it a petition for relief under any chapter or provision of the Bankruptcy laws of the United States, as amended from time to time (and in the case of any involuntary proceeding the same is not dismissed within sixty (60) days thereof).

THEN, upon the occurrence of any such Event of Default, or upon the expiration of the term of this Note, Holder at its election, and without presentment, demand, notice of any kind, all of which are expressly waived by Maker, may declare the entire outstanding balance of principal and interest thereon immediately due and payable, together with all costs of collection, including attorneys' fees, and/or may exercise upon or enforce its rights to its Collateral, as are set forth in this Agreement.

NO WAIVER BY HOLDER

The acceptance by Holder of any payment under this Note after the date such payment is due, or the failure to declare an Event of Default as herein provided, shall not constitute a waiver of any of the terms of this Note or the right to require the prompt payment when due of future or succeeding payments or to declare an Event of Default for any failure to so pay or for any other default. The acceptance by Holder of a payment of a portion of any installment at any time that such installment is due in full shall not cure or excuse the default caused by the failure to pay such installment in full and shall not constitute a waiver of the right to require full payment when due of all future or succeeding installments.

ATTORNEYS' FEES AND COSTS

The prevailing party in any legal dispute concerning this Note shall be entitled to seek immediate reimbursement for reasonable attorneys' fees and all other costs and expenses so incurred.

WAIVERS

Maker, endorsers, guarantors and sureties of this Note hereby waive diligence, demand, presentment, notice of non-payment, protest and notice of protest; expressly agree that this Note, or any payment hereunder, may be renewed, modified or extended from time to time and at any time; and consent to the acceptance or release of security for this Note or the release of any party or guarantor, all without in any way affecting their liability and waive the right to plead any and all statutes of limitations as a defense to any demand on this Note, or on any guaranty thereof, or to any agreement to pay the same to the full extent permissible by law.

to cover the Initial Advance and/or the Home Rental Advances in connection with such Cancelled Show. Unless otherwise defined herein, the capitalized terms shall have the meanings ascribed to them in the Tour Agreement.

Any payment hereunder shall be applied first to the payment of costs and charges of collection, if any, then to accrued interest, if any, and the balance, if any, shall be then applied to reduction of principal. Principal and interest are payable in lawful money of the United States of America.

SECURITY AGREEMENT -- COLLATERAL OWNED BY ARTISTCO ONLY – ARTIST IS NOT PLEDGING ANY COLLATERAL

To secure the faithful and timely performance of each Maker's obligations hereunder and each Maker's obligations under the Artist Agreement, and all extensions, modifications, substitutions, replacements, and renewals of all such obligations (collectively, the "Secured Obligations"), Artistco hereby assigns and grants to Holder, a security interest in Artistco's right, title and interest in, to, and under the following properties, assets and rights, wherever located, whether now owned or hereafter acquired or arising, and all proceeds and products thereof (all of the same being hereinafter referred to collectively as, the "Collateral"): contract rights, the right to the payment of money in which Artistco has an interest, insurance claims and proceeds, commercial tort claims, securities and all other investment property, and all general intangibles (including all accounts receivable and payment intangibles). Artistco shall cooperate in Holder's efforts to perfect the security interest granted to Holder hereunder. To the extent allowed by law, Artistco hereby irrevocably appoints Holder, acting singly, as Artistco's attorney-in-fact, with full authority in the place and stead of Artistco and in the name of Artistco, or otherwise, from time to time in Holder's discretion, if a Default shall have occurred and be continuing, to take any action and to execute any instrument that Holder may deem necessary or advisable to accomplish the purposes of this agreement, including, without limitation:

(a) to ask, demand, collect, sue for, recover, compound, receive, and give acquittance and receipts for, money due and to become due under or in respect of any of the Collateral;

(b) to receive, endorse, and collect any drafts or other instruments and documents in connection with the foregoing;

(c) to file claims or take any action or institute any proceedings that Holder may deem necessary or desirable for the collection of any of the Collateral or otherwise to enforce the rights of Holder with respect to any of the Collateral; and

(d) to file one or more financing or continuation statements, and amendments thereof, relative to all or any part of the Collateral without the signature of the Holder where permitted by law.

DEFAULT/ACCELERATION

If any one or more of the following events shall occur (hereinafter called an "Event of Default"), namely:

Exhibit C

PROMISSORY NOTE

January 2̲6̲, 2009

U.S. $6,200,000
Los Angeles, California

FOR VALUE RECEIVED, the undersigned, The Michael Jackson Company, LLC, a Delaware limited liability company ("Artistco") and Michael Jackson ("Artist"), an individual residing in California (together, "Maker"), promises to pay, on a joint and several basis, to AEG Live LLC ("Holder" or "Promoter"), or order, at ████████████████████████████████ or at such place as Holder may from time to time designate, the principal amount of Six Million Two Hundred Thousand United States Dollars (U.S. $6,200,000), with interest on such amount until paid, at the rate set forth below and payable as follows:

INTEREST RATE

The amount of outstanding principal shall bear **no interest** unless the full principal amount owing is not timely paid within five (5) business days after the Maturity Date (defined below) or within five (5) business days after written notice of Maker's failure to pay the full principal amount owing on or before the Maturity Date, whichever is later, in which event simple, non-compounding interest shall accrue on the principal balance owing from and after the execution of this Promissory Note ("Note") by Maker at the rate of ten percent (10%) per annum, and shall be calculated on the basis of a 365-day year.

TERM

The term of this Note shall be from the date of this Note through and including the earlier of (a) six months after the last Show of the first leg of the Tour under the Tour Agreement (defined below) but in no event later than December 31, 2009 or (b) six months after Promoter makes a written request for such payment, if ever, in accordance with Paragraph 4.2.5 of the Tour Agreement (defined below), (such earlier date shall be referred to as the "Maturity Date"), at which time all unpaid principal shall be due. The parties may renew the term and extend the Maturity Date by signing a written modification of this Note extending such dates, and shall do so if required by the terms of the Tour Agreement.

PAYMENT

Principal shall be due and payable in full on the Maturity Date; provided that the principal amount owing shall be reduced by an amount equal to the sum of (i) the portions of the Initial Advance and Home Rental Advances which are Earned by the Artist under the terms of the Tour Agreement dated January 26, 2009 and executed by and between Promoter, Artistco and Artist regarding the worldwide concert tour of Artist (the "Tour Agreement"); (ii) any repayment by Artistco and/or Artist of the Home Rental Advances accomplished by replacing the letter of credit delivered by Promoter to the landlord of the Bel Air home and causing such letter of credit to be cancelled as permitted under Paragraph 4.2.2 of the Tour Agreement, and (iii) with respect to any Show that is cancelled (a "Cancelled Show"), any amount paid to Promoter in its capacity as a loss payee under cancellation insurance obtained by Artistco

Exhibit B

Inducement Letter – Michael Jackson

As a further inducement to AEG Live LLC ("Promoter") to enter into the foregoing Artist Agreement with The Michael Jackson Company, LLC ("Artistco") dated January 26, 2009 (such agreement including the exhibits thereto being referred to collectively as the "Agreement"), it being to the undersigned's benefit that Promoter do so, and in consideration of the execution thereof by Promoter, the undersigned hereby:

1. Guarantees the full performance by Artistco of all of Artistco's obligations under the Agreement, and agrees to be jointly and severally liable for all such obligations;

2. Represents and warrants that Artistco has the right to enter into the Agreement and to assume all of the obligations, warranties and undertakings to Promoter on the part of Artistco contained therein, and that Artistco shall continue to have those rights until all of those obligations, warranties and undertakings shall have been fully performed and discharged;

3. Represents and warrants that all of the representations, warranties and agreements on the part of Artistco contained in the Agreement that concern Artistco and/or the undersigned are and shall remain true and correct, and the undersigned agrees to be bound thereby;

4. Agrees that the undersigned's liability hereunder is direct and immediate, is not conditioned upon the pursuit by Promoter of any remedy Promoter may have against Artistco, and is secured by the collateral identified Paragraph 16.3 of the Agreement, which section is incorporated herein by this reference, and that the terms hereof are irrevocable, and any proceeding against the undersigned may be brought pursuant to the forum selection and choice of law provisions contained in the Agreement;

5. Waives any rights of subrogation, reimbursement, indemnification, and contribution and any other rights and defenses that are or may become available to the undersigned by reason of California Civil Code Sections 2787 to 2855, inclusive, and further agrees that such waivers are intended by the undersigned to be effective to the maximum extent permitted by Section 2856 of the California Civil Code; and

6. Facsimile copies or photocopies of signature of this inducement letter shall be as valid as original.

_____
Michael Jackson

CHAPTER THIRTEEN

DR. CONRAD MURRAY

Dr. Conrad Murray

D r. Conrad Murray is a physician licensed to practice medicine in the State of California. He also engaged in the practice of medicine in the county of Los Angeles where he was treating Michael Jackson. Dr. Murray has given contradictory versions of the times and events which led to Michael Jackson's death. Each contradiction in my opinion shows a reckless disregard for the life of Michael Jackson. He changed dates and times, and he also failed to keep medical records which were a violation of California's Board of Medicine.

Dr. Murray's Deception

On June 25th, 2009, at 12:22 p.m., the Los Angeles fire department received a 911 call from Alberto Alvarez who was Michael Jackson's security agent at his home in Beverly Hills. He stated that a fifty year-old gentleman was not breathing and that he needed emergency assistance. Alvarez did not state the address of the location, and he did not identify the gentleman to whom he was referring. Alvarez said the patient was under the care of a doctor who was administering CPR on the bed. The 911 operator said the patient should be moved to the floor. The operator said CPR should be continued under the doctor's care, and the paramedics were on the way. The fire department immediately responded to the 911 call. The paramedics arrived at 100 N. Carolwood within four minutes at 12:26 p.m. They were at Michael's bedside at 12:27 p.m. Michael was not breathing, his color was pale, and he was in cardiac arrest. The state of his condition was serious. His pupils were fixed and dilated, and he had no detectable pulse or respiration.

Dr. Murray falsely told the Los Angeles fire department and paramedics that he had administered one thousand cubic centimeters of Lorazepam (Ativan) to Michael. He told them he had administered no other drugs. These statements were false, and Dr. Murray knew they were false at the time they were made. I feel he made the statements to conceal his violations of the law for the over-administration of dangerous drugs to Michael, and Dr. Murray also violated the law which prohibits false statements to a medical technician engaged in life-saving activity.

The truth of the matter was that Dr. Murray had administered not only Lorazepam (Ativan) to Michael, but he had also administered a lethal dose of Propofol, a fast-acting hypnotic used for general anesthesia and surgical procedures in a hospital setting. Also Dr. Murray had administered a total of nine different drugs to Michael: Propofol, Lidocaine, Diazepam, Nordiazepam, Lorazepam, Midazolam, Ephedrine, Flumazenil, and Flomax. Dr. Murray's statement to the paramedics, who were relying upon him to attempt to save Michael's life, in my opinion demonstrates a total reckless disregard for and endangerment of Michael's life, which impaired their rescue efforts to save him. This is why I totally believe that Dr. Conrad Murray should have been charged with murder.

At 12:29 p.m., the paramedics started their resuscitation. Michael had no pulse, blood pressure, or oxygen saturation reading. His heart was not contracting nor was he breathing. Michael's condition remained unchanged throughout the resuscitation except that at 12:34 p.m., the pulse less electrical activity had ceased, and there was no heartbeat.

The paramedics administered several cardiac-stimulating drugs without effort. At 12:50 p.m., the paramedics contacted UCLA Medical Center, and described the absence of any signs of life coming from Michael Jackson. Dr. Richelle Cooper, who was head of the UCLA Emergency Department, told the paramedics to consider terminating their resuscitation efforts.

Dr. Murray stated to the paramedics that he would be responsible for further resuscitation efforts. The paramedics then placed Michael in the ambulance at 1:07 p.m., and the paramedics again attempted resuscitation without success. The ambulance arrived at UCLA Medical Center at 1:13 p.m. Throughout the entire resuscitation effort, Dr. Murray concealed the drugs he had administered to Michael. At 1:15 p.m., the paramedics brought Michael into the UCLA Emergency Room. In Dr. Murray's presence Michael was identified to the UCLA personnel under the false name Soule Shaun. The attendants noticed that while there was a cardiologist at the scene, he provided no medical history. This was a total violation of the normal standards of care. Michael arrived with no pulse, blood pressure, spontaneous respirations, or heartbeat. He was given several drugs including Dopamine, Epinephrine, Atropine, Vasopressin, and Sodium Bicarbonate, and his breathing was assisted by bagging with oxygen. He was not alert, his pupils were fixed and dilated, and he had no response to pain.

Dr. Richelle Cooper, the head of UCLA Center Emergency Department, spoke to Dr. Murray. Dr. Murray told Dr. Cooper he had felt a pulse from Michael when he had discovered that he was not breathing. He stated he had only administered Lorazepam, Valium, and Flomax. Dr. Murray said nothing about Propofol and nothing about Flumazenil or the other drugs found in Michael's body at his autopsy. Dr. Murray's conduct was far away from the standard of care. He demonstrated a reckless disregard for Michael Jackson's life by concealing the Propofol and the other drugs he had been administering to him for months.

Dr. Richelle Cooper's written report dated June 26th, 2009, stated as follows: *"The initial limited history was provided by*

Dr. Murray, during the resuscitation of the patient, and is noted in brief on the medical record. By report of Dr. Murray the patient had been working long hours but had not been ill. There was no reported trauma or seizure activity preceding the arrest. The only reported medications reported for the patient were Valium and Flomax. There was no history of drug use by the patient as reported by Dr. Murray."

The events surrounding the arrest reported by Dr. Murray were that he had inserted an IV and had given Michael two milligrams of Lorazepam in an IV sometime earlier that day. Dr. Murray administered a second two milligrams of an IV dose of Lorazepam and reported witnessing Michael's cardiac arrest. Dr. Murray's statements to Dr. Cooper were outrageous. Dr. Murray's statements appeared to be false and misleading to emergency personnel. Michael had been ill; this was also not reported to the emergency personnel.

Dr. Murray's Contradictory Statements to the Police

On June 27th, 2009, two days after Michael died; Dr. Murray told the police he was afraid Michael was addicted to Propofol. He said that Michael had a long history of addiction and he was trying to wean him off the drugs. Dr. Murray told Dr. Cooper on the day Michael died, that Michael had no history of drug use. Dr. Murray's history of drug prescription to Michael Jackson went back to December 2008. When the police searched Michael's home following his death, they seized dozens of drug vials showing Michael's extreme drug use. Some of the vials showed that on December 22nd, 2008, Dr. Murray prescribed Temazepam to Michael. On April 28th, 2009, he prescribed Lorazepam to Michael. On May 14th, 2009, he also prescribed Lidocaine to Michael. Yet Dr. Murray told Dr. Cooper that Michael had no history of drug use. Moreover, Dr.

Murray told Dr. Cooper that Michael had not been ill. However, aside from Michael's addiction illness, Michael was also suffering at the time of his death from "co-mobilities," including: anemia, chronic pneumonia, chronic bronchitis, and also brain swelling. In my opinion, Dr. Conrad Murray's statements to Dr. Cooper were a blatant fabrication designed to conceal his reckless behavior.

The Emergency Room's Resuscitation Efforts

At 1:21 p.m., the nurses and physicians at UCLA detected a weak pulse and cardiac activity in Michael. At 1:22 p.m. he showed heart activity. Dr. Cooper reported that when Michael was intubated with an endotracheal tube he had good breath sounds and the initial cardiac heart rhythms appeared to be wide and slow. At 1:52 p.m., he had a pulse of fifty-three beats per minute. At 2:05 p.m., the physicians inserted a balloon pump to attempt resuscitation and obtain circulation with a spontaneous heart beat. The pump was placed in the aorta just above the heart, and his blood pressure between heart beats went from twenty to approximately forty at times and sometimes to sixty. Despite these efforts Michael did not regain a spontaneous pulse or heartbeat. Following the failure of the balloon pump to restore circulation, and the lack of a heartbeat, pulse, and spontaneous respirations, Michael was pronounced dead at 2:26 p.m. on June 25th, 2009.

Dr. Murray Concealed Information

From Police at the Hospital

Dr. Murray met with the police who were investigating the case at UCLA Medical Center. He gave them the same story, concealing the fact that he had administered the drug Propofol and the numerous other drugs he gave to Michael. He concealed information from the police in the same manner he concealed information from paramedics and the emergency room doctors. The day following Michael Jackson's death, on June 26th, 2009, the police searched the Carolwood home and seized eight used bottles of Propofol, and later another three. They seized medication from Michael's bedside table that included Clonazepam, Benoquin, Flomax, Hydroquinone, Lidocaine, Temazepam, Tizanidine, Trazodone, Flumazenil, Ephedrine, Prednisone, Amoxicillin, Azithromycin, Lorazepam, Midazolam, and Valium. The police also found several baggies of marijuana, Latnaoprost flush solution, which is used to control glaucoma, a box of Nystatin, an anti-fungal drug used to treat yeast infections, and Triamcinolone which is a topical steroid to treat skin inflammation. The Clonazepam and Trazodone were prescribed by Dr. Metzger. The Tizanidine was prescribed by Dr. Klein.

According to the court documents, Dr. Murray did not disclose any of these drugs to the paramedics except Ativan. He did not disclose any of these drugs to the doctors except Valium, Ativan, and Flomax. In my opinion, Dr. Murray concealed his deadly use of Propofol for the sole purpose of protecting himself from an accusation of improper use of medications for Michael, knowing all along that Michael Jackson's life was on the line. Dr. Murray falsely stated three times the nature of the drugs that he administered to Michael. Three times he misled authorities concerning his unlawful actions. In my opinion, he engaged in a reckless pattern of not only treating Michael Jackson with total disregard for his safety, but also making false statements about his treatment over and over again to authorities.

Dr. Murray's Story Told to Police

On June 27th, 2009, which was two days after Michael died, Dr. Murray, his attorneys, and advisors met with Los Angeles

Police Department detectives. Dr. Murray appeared at their request. Prior to this meeting he had consulted with his attorney before making his statements to the police, after which he claimed his statements were incorrect. Dr. Murray told police he gave fifty milligrams of diluted Propofol, with an unspecified amount of Lidocaine, administered by IV to Michael, each night for six weeks. He claimed he had been treating Michael for insomnia. The Propofol helped Michael sleep. Dr. Murray claimed he felt Michael may have been forming an addiction, and therefore was attempting to wean Michael off of the drug. His weaning process involved giving Michael on June 22nd, 2009, three days before his death, twenty-five milligrams of Propofol, along with an unknown amount of Lorazepam and Midazolam. Dr. Murray claimed Michael was able to sleep with this combination. On June 23rd, 2009, Dr. Murray claimed he gave Michael Lorazepam and Midazolam without any Propofol.

On June 25th, 2009, the date of Michael's death, Dr. Murray claimed he arrived at the Carolwood house at 1:00 a.m. Michael had been rehearsing at the Staples Center in downtown Los Angeles until midnight. Before Michael left rehearsals, Dr. Murray claimed he received a call from Michael's associates requesting he go to the Carolwood house to attend to Michael. Dr. Murray told the police that Michael was complaining of not feeling well, he was suffering from dehydration, and had not been able to sleep. Dr. Murray said at 1:30 a.m. he attempted to induce sleep by giving Michael a 10 milligram tablet of Valium. Thirty minutes later at 2:00 a.m., Michael still had not gone to sleep. Dr. Murray then administered an injection of 2 milligrams of Lorazepam, with an unknown substance. At 3:00 a.m., Dr. Murray administered two milligrams of Midazolam, and he also stated he administered another 2 milligrams of Lorazepam with an unknown substance. Dr. Murray claimed that Michael remained awake for the next two and a half hours.

At 7:30 a.m., Dr. Murray administered yet another 2 milligrams of Midazolam through an IV. He claimed he was continuously at Michael's bedside and was monitoring him with a pulse oximeter. However, when the police searched Michael's house, they found the pulse oximeter in the closet in the next room.

At 10:40 a.m., Dr. Murray claimed he administered 25 milligrams of Propofol diluted with Lidocaine through the IV drip. He said Michael finally went to sleep. But now we know this was the fatal dose that would kill Michael. Dr. Murray claimed ten minutes later he left Michael's beside to go to the restroom. He claimed he was only out of the room for approximately two minutes. At 10:52 a.m., he said he returned to Michael's bedside and noticed that Michael was no longer breathing. He said he started CPR, and also administered 2/10 of a milligram of Flumazenil to Michael, which is an anti-overdose medication, which has no effect on Propofol. In addition, the dose was inadequate for the Lorazepam, which was improperly administered. Evidently, Dr. Murray did not know how to use this drug. Any normal person would have called the paramedics in that instant. It was grossly negligent and reckless of him not to have done so.

Dr. Murray claimed he called the security guard, Michael Amir Williams (Brother Mike) on his cell phone for help. He claimed when he told Williams what was happening, he did not respond in a helpful manner. Dr. Murray also claimed he continued to perform CPR.

A few minutes later Dr. Murray claimed he rushed downstairs to the kitchen and asked the chef, Kai Chase, to send Prince Michael, Michael's, twelve year-old son upstairs to his father's room. I can't imagine why Dr. Murray would want Michael's twelve year-old son to witness his father dying. *How cruel is that?* After returning to Michael's room he claimed he continued the CPR on the bed. Being a medically trained physician, Dr. Murray should have known that Michael should have been moved to a hard surface to conduct the CPR properly. When Prince Michael entered the room, Dr. Murray immediately asked for assistance from the security. Alberto Alvarez told the police that before he called 911, Dr. Murray instructed him to conceal the bottles of Propofol by placing them into a bag. It is outrageous that Dr. Murray would stop performing CPR to clean up the room so that the medications would not be discovered by anyone. Dr. Murray also placed the previously unused wires of the pulse oximeter on Michael's fingers before the paramedics arrived. Alberto Alvarez stated to the police that he was only allowed to call 911 after the drugs were hidden.

Michael stopped breathing at 10:52 a.m., but the Los Angeles Fire Department has the recorded time of the 911 call listed at 12:22 p.m., which is approximately one hour and thirty minutes later. Dr. Murray told the detectives several times that it was around 11:00 a.m., that he found Michael not breathing. Regardless, if he discovered him not breathing at 10:52 a.m., or 11:00 a.m., he still did not call the paramedics until 12:22 p.m. Why did it take him so long? Any logical person whether they had a medical degree or not, would have called 911 *while* performing CPR. During that time Dr. Murray did make three calls, which of course he concealed from the police. These other calls consumed forty-seven minutes of talk time according to his cell phone records. If Dr. Murray could make these other calls, why in the world did he not call the paramedics first? What else could have been more important? If the paramedics could have gotten there sooner, Michael might be alive today.

Dr. Murray's Revised Version of Events

When Dr. Murray discovered that there were telephone and

other records that exposed his outrageous actions, he claimed, despite his interview with the Los Angeles Police on June 27th, 2009, he got his story wrong. He then altered his story in an attempt to cover up his claims about the telephone records the police obtained. The reason Dr. Murray felt he could change his story is because he didn't keep any medical records concerning the treatment he provided to Michael.

The search warrant affidavit of Los Angeles Detective Daniel Myers dated November 13th, 2009, stated: "The searches of Dr. Murray's residence and business failed to yield any notes, patient profiles, treatment history, records, and charts regarding the treatment for Michael Joseph Jackson at his residence at 100 North Carolwood Drive."

Dr. Murray's new version of the story meant that his old version was yet the fourth time he created a false version of events. Dr. Murray's new version was the fifth time he falsely stated what happened. He has lied so many times, which version are we suppose to believe? But one thing is clear…the new version again concealed his reckless administration of the life-threatening drugs he gave to Michael. Dr. Murray claimed in his new version that he discovered Michael was not breathing while he was on the phone with his girlfriend at 12:05 p.m. If you notice, the story changed from him going to the bathroom for two minutes and then observing Michael at 10:40 a.m., to him talking on the phone with several people from 11:18 a.m. to 12:05 p.m. for forty-seven minutes. Dr. Murray stopped his observations of Michael and substituted telephone conversations with others which caused him not to notice that Michael had stopped breathing. Dr. Murray's conduct under this new version of the story was even more dangerous and negligent than the first account of what happened. The administration of the Propofol requires a measured infusion using a mechanical pump which is supposed to be constantly monitored because of the unpredictable changes in the patient's blood pressure. Instead, Dr. Murray infused the drug by IV drip and syringe without any monitoring or resuscitation equipment, rendering it inherently dangerous. Michael's life, in my opinion, was recklessly endangered by Dr. Murray talking on the phone outside of Michael's presence for forty-seven minutes while a Propofol drip infusion took place. This probably explains why he didn't even notice that Michael had stopped breathing. There isn't any evidence available that would prove that he monitored Michael after he administered the Propofol. Dr. Murray is a highly educated man. He should have known that an autopsy would be performed and the drugs he gave Michael would be discovered, as would his telephone records. It makes me wonder what else he is hiding and who he is protecting.

Dr. Murray's Reckless Conduct and the Dangers Involved by his Concealment

On June 25th, 2009, prior to treating Michael, Dr. Murray attended a strip club called Sam's Hofbrau in Los Angeles. He consumed alcohol which was reckless of him to do just before giving the anesthesia to Michael. Dr. Murray concealed the fact that he had been drinking from Michael. Dr. Murray failed to explain to Michael the risks and the benefits where the Propofol was concerned, not to mention the fact he never obtained Michael's written consent to administer the drug. Dr. Murray put Michael's life in jeopardy by concealing from Michael the dangers where this drug was concerned. It seems that Dr. Murray held little regard for human life by concealing the dangers of the drug and by violating the standards of care that all physicians have to follow.

Dr. Murray Withholds Information
Concerning the Drug Propofol

Dr. Murray did not have in his possession any sort of traceable number to order the Propofol or any of the other drugs he administered to Michael. We do know that he purchased the drugs from Applied Pharmacy in Las Vegas without using Michael's name and had the drugs shipped to his girlfriend's house in Santa Monica, California. Dr. Murray, I truly believe, thought he could conceal his actions and prevent police officers, physicians, and family members from discovering the truth. Dr. Murray secretly obtained the drugs without the authorities knowing for his own personal gain under conditions that threatened and ultimately took Michael's life.

Dr. Murray Recklessly Covered up Hazardous
Prescription Drug Interactions

It appears that Dr. Murray gave Michael drugs with careless neglect, because the drugs he gave him had life-threatening interactions. Dr. Murray gave Michael the Propofol fully knowing the drug had adverse interactions with Valium, Ativan, and Midazolam, all of which he gave to Michael the day he died. I guess this lethal combination was a toxic cocktail. From what I understand, Propofol interacts adversely with Ephedrine (which keeps you awake) and Nordiazepam, both of which the coroner found in Michael's system. Dr. Murray knew that Michael had taken these drugs which were contraindicated with drugs Dr. Murray administered. Dr. Murray tried to conceal the fact that these drugs were dangerous when they interacted together. His conduct was an excessive deviation from the standard of care all doctors take an oath to uphold. In essence, Dr. Conrad Murray acted with complete disregard for Michael's life and his well-being.

The Coroner's Findings

On June 26th, 2009, the coroner's office conducted an autopsy on Michael, and reached conclusions from the autopsy on September 18th, 2009. The report showed that Michael did in fact die from acute Propofol intoxication, contributed to by what is known as the "Benzodiazepine Effect." Michael also had what is called a "polypharmacy" of drugs in his system meaning he was using multiple medications. There were a total of seven different drugs detected in the toxicology screen. Two of the drugs, Flumazenil, and Flomax were detected in the IV. One of them, Propofol showed lethal levels in Michael's body. Dr. Murray stated he only gave Michael 25 milligrams of Propofol on June 25th, 2009. Nevertheless, the coroner's toxicology report showed lethal quantities in his system where the administration of the drug exceeded more than five times that amount. The presence of the lethal amounts of Propofol in Michael's body exposes yet another untruth on Dr. Murray's part. His actions not only endangered Michael's life, but brought it to an end.

The toxicology report also showed that Michael had Propofol in the clear gel that fills the globe of the eye between the retina and the lens. The presence of the drug in this area shows that it was given to Michael several hours prior to his death. In my opinion, this proves beyond a reasonable doubt that everything Dr. Murray has said is a complete and utter lie.

Dr. Murray Disregarded Michael's Brain, Lung, and Anemia Symptoms

At the UCLA Emergency Room, Dr. Murray told Dr. Cooper that prior to June 25th, 2009, Michael had not been sick. However, Michael was suffering from chronic pneumonia, chronic respiratory bronchitis, anemia, and brain swelling. The

Los Angeles County Coroner's autopsy report documented that Michael had underlying illnesses. Dr. Conrad Murray's gross negligence in giving Michael benzodiazepines and Propofol while not treating his co-morbidity conditions was an extreme departure from the medical standard of care, and in my opinion, was very reckless on his part.

Michael had neurological, pulmonary, and anemia signs several weeks before his death. In May and June of 2009, Michael was confused and easily frightened. He had impaired memory, and he was obsessive and also disoriented at times. He had a loss of appetite and very little energy. He was cold and shivering during the summer rehearsals for his show, which is shown in photos and videos of him wearing heavy clothes while the other dancers were scantily clad and sweating. Other people loaned him jackets and shirts to keep him warm, and he requested a heater to control the shivering.

Dr. Murray's continuous "polypharmacy" drug administration along with the Propofol every night as a sleep aid in the presence of Michael's "co-morbidity conditions was reckless". Dr. Murray ignored the signs of Michael's pulmonary inflammation, brain swelling, and anemia. Carelessly, he continued his drug treatment in spite of the effect of the "polypharmacy" and benzodiazepines. His actions brought forth an extreme separation from the standard of care. Recklessly he showed blatant disregard for Michael's life, by administering a "polypharmacy," which included benzodiazepines and Propofol, while fully knowing the dangers.

Summary of Allegations

In my opinion Dr. Murray concealed his own wrongdoings to save himself instead of Michael's life. What Dr. Conrad Murray did was a complete obstruction of justice and reckless endangerment that ultimately cost Michael his life. Dr. Murray lied time and time again. He violated federal and state laws regarding the administration of various drugs to Michael.

Dr. Murray violated federal and state laws as follows:

1) Giving false information to emergency personnel
2) Excessive treatment or prescribing medications not documented in the patient's medical records
3) Failure to report the procedures conducted outside of the acute care hospital that resulted in death
4) Gross, and repeated negligence, incompetence, and acts involving dishonesty
5) Prescribing and treating an addict which is prohibited by Health and Safety Rules and Regulations
6) Prescribing and Furnishing dangerous drugs without medical indication
7) Failure to maintain accurate patient records
8) Failure to keep records of substances in Comprehensive Drug, Health, and Safety Code

Dr. Murray violated his medical oath when he illegally prescribed and over administered so many different kinds of drugs to Michael. I honestly feel that Dr. Murray is a part of the cover up and conspiracy behind Michael's death. There is no charge in my opinion that fits his actions other than murder.

CHAPTER FOURTEEN

REVIEW OF THE FRAUDULENT WILL

The Fraudulent Will

Shortly after Michael's burial I received a call from his younger brother, Randy Jackson.

He said, "Rowe, I need to talk to you for a minute."

I said, "About what?"

He said, "About the will that John Branca has presented."

I replied, "What about the will?"

He said, "I truly believe that the will is a fake."

I asked the question, "What would make you think that?"

He said to me, "The will was allegedly signed by Michael on July 7th, 2002, at 5 p.m. in Los Angeles, California."

I replied, "What is wrong with that?"

He said, "I don't think Michael was in Los Angeles on July 7th, 2002."

I asked, "Where was he?"

He said "I think he was in New York. If I'm not mistaken, I think this was the week when Michael and Al Sharpton were picketing Tommy Mottola (ex-president of Sony Records)." He then said, "I have asked Rev. Al Sharpton for a copy of the tape so that I could be sure."

We began discussing and investigating this on a daily basis. About three days later, Randy said he had received the tape, and Michael was indeed in New York on July 7, 2002. He was not in Los Angeles where John Branca and John McClain reported he signed the will. Randy told me that he had gotten attorney Brian Oxman to assist us in the investigation.

On July 7th, 2002, Michael Jackson was in New York City, not in Los Angeles at five o'clock to sign the alleged will. Branca and McClain have hidden from the court a material fact, that Michael Jackson did not sign the purported will dated July 7th, 2002 as they claimed he did. Concealing this information is a fraud, and should disqualify them from being the executors of Michael's estate. Branca and McClain had a duty to inform the court that Michael Jackson was not in Los Angeles on July 7th, 2002, but he was instead in New York. This fact concerning the alleged will has been concealed from the public and the court. Branca and McClain have violated their duties by testifying under penalty of perjury on at least seventeen occasions. They testified that the purported will of July 7th, 2002, was correct.

1) They testified on July 1st, 2009, for a petition to probate the will.

2) July 23rd, 2009, application for family allowance.

3) July 29th, 2009, application for proposed book deal.

4) July 31st, 2009, response and objection to petition for letter of administration by Joseph and Katherine Jackson.

5) July 31st, 2009, first supplement to petition for probate.

6) August 3rd, 2009, supplement to probate petition.

7) August 3rd, 2009, petition to make payment to Michael Laperruque for contract with Michael's Jackson Company dated May 30th, 2008.

8) September 17th, 2009, application for order authorizing supplement agreement.

9) September 20th, 2009, application to enter publishing agreement.

10) September 20th, 2009, application to enter merchandising agreement.

11) September 20th, 2009, application to enter business agreement Opus.

12) September 22nd, 2009, application to enter business transaction Bravado.

13) September 28th, 2009, application to enter business transaction.

14) September 28th, 2009, application to enter contract with Columbia Pictures.

15) September 28th, 2009, application to enter into publishing agreement.

16) September 28th, 2009 motion to enter book publishing agreement.

17) September 29th, 2009, application to enter agreement digital distribution of audio.

Branca and McClain were grossly negligent in their statements to the court. They have concealed information from the court that should have them removed as trustees. They have also conducted themselves in a fraudulent and deceptive manner. In my opinion, they should not be trusted to oversee the Michael Jackson Estate. Both of them should be disqualified and charges should be brought against them for fraud. My reasoning is Michael Jackson terminated John Branca as his attorney on February 3, 2003. In a written termination letter (see Letter in this chapter), Michael Jackson instructed John Branca to resign from all positions he had in Michael's personal and business life. Branca failed to follow Michael Jackson's instructions and neglected to remove himself as executor of Michael Jackson Family Trust.

On February 3rd, 2003, Michael instructed Branca to turn over to his new attorneys all records, files, and papers dealing with his personal and business life. While Branca turned over his other files, Branca secretly refused to turn over the purported July 7th, 2002, will and March 2002 trust. No will was ever turned over to Michael's new attorney. This was a total violation of Branca's fiduciary duty as Michael's lawyers. Branca concealed the will, and concealed his refusal to resign as executor. Branca's concealment and failure to resign continued for many years despite Michael's numerous demands that Branca turn over all documents and resign from all positions. Conduct of this nature should not be allowed by the courts. This was a total violation not only to Michael Jackson, but to his children. In 2003, Michael Jackson launched an investigation into Branca's alleged embezzlement activities, regarding Michael's money. The investigators, the firm of Interfor in New York reported in February, March, and a final report on April 15th, 2003, that there was an improper relationship between Tommy Mottola and John Branca whereby Branca and Mottola were allegedly funneling Michael's money to offshore accounts in the Caribbean. The Interfor report caused Michael Jackson great anguish and Michael demanded that Branca was never to have anything to do with him, his business, his family, or his personal life again.

Michael terminated John Branca because of his belief that Branca had committed crimes against him. Branca never gave Michael an accounting of whether this report was true or false, nor did he disclose his books and records to Michael.

Michael Jackson's belief that this occurred was the basis for Branca's termination. Branca never complied with Michael's demand that he make an accounting and resign.

For many years, John Branca entered into thousands of licensing agreements with the public for music and songs on behalf of Michael Jackson and the Sony/ATV Trust. Michael terminated Branca because he believed Branca was embezzling money from these licensing arrangements. Neither Branca nor his firm has been audited concerning the multi-million dollar proceeds and receipts of these transactions. Branca cannot make an independent audit of himself while serving as executor. When Branca filed the petition for probate on July 1st, 2009, less than a week after Michael passed, he failed to disclose his prior business relationship with Michael Jackson regarding licensing and the Sony/ATV Trust. It is not a question of the truthfulness or accuracy of the investigators report or even Michael Jackson's belief. Rather, it is a matter of following Michael's instructions to resign, turn over all documents, and terminate all relationships. Branca refused to obey his client Michael Jackson's instructions. Branca should now be made to follow his instructions, resign as executor and he should be prosecuted to the fullest extent of the law.

Michael Jackson also signed various attorney retainer agreements with his law firm from 1993 to 1995. In those agreements Branca took five percent of the proceeds of Michael Jackson's businesses and performances, and then, without further entitlement, a five percent ownership in Michael's Sony/ATV Catalogue royalties, all of which were the subject matter of his representation.

These contracts for representation not only constitute a conflict of interest, but also violate Branca's duty as a lawyer by taking an interest in the subject matter of the representation without his client's authorization. Michael told me, in 2004 that his Sony/ATV Catalogue was valued in excess of $1 billion. A 5% interest represents $50 million. There was no conflict of interest disclosure in the retainer agreement. Michael did not have independent counsel to review this transaction. Branca's representation thereafter was tainted by the continued conflicts of interests and concealment of his actions that allowed him to continue taking advantage of Michael.

In April 2006, Michael Jackson paid Branca $15 million to get back his five percent interest in the Sony/ATV Catalogue. When Branca filed his petition to be the executor of Michael's estate, he conveniently concealed this multi-million dollar transaction and material profiting from, what I truly believe to be, the stolen 5% interest in Michael's business. Branca had a duty to disclose to the court the nature, amount, and details behind this transaction. He violated his duty as an attorney to give full disclosure to the court of Michael's payment of $15 million dollars to Branca in 2006 to reclaim his 5% interest in the Sony/ATV catalogue is a total conflict of interest with the Estate of Michael Jackson. Because Branca is the special administrator and designated executor, Branca has not and will not seek sanctions against himself; thereby perpetrating an intentional fraud upon the court. And now, he sits at the "throne of Michael's estate". What kind of world are we living in? I truly feel that this is being accomplished because of a corrupt judicial system in Los Angeles County, California. I am sure that Michael would not approve of John Branca and John McClain being co-executors of his estate. Barry Siegel was also listed as an executor to Michael's will. On August 26th, 2003, Siegel resigned as executor of Michael's will. He sent his letter of resignation to Branca. John Branca concealed that document until he filed the July 1st, 2009, probate petition, and this is in violation of Michael's instructions to resign all positions and turn over all documents as he requested him to do in February 2003.

When Branca filed the probate petition on July 1st, 2009, he attached the August 26th, 2003, Siegel letter. Barry Siegel resigned pursuant to the termination letter from Michael similar to the letter Branca received. However, while Siegel complied with Michael's instructions and resigned, Branca did not. When Branca filed his probate petition he concealed the fact that Barry Siegel had followed Michael's instructions but he had not. Branca had a duty to disclose to the court and to present the Siegel resignation letter of August 26th, 2003. Branca's petition to be executor violates Michael Jackson's termination letter of February 2003. When Michael terminated Branca on February

3rd, 2003, and requested that he turn over all documents to his new attorney, Branca never turned over a reported July 7th, 2002, will. This is a complete violation and my true opinion is that John Branca should be removed from Michael Jackson's estate and immediately be prosecuted.

On October 21st, 2009, Randy Jackson called a meeting at his sister Janet's home in the Century City area of Los Angeles. This meeting was to present to everyone involved (which was just a few) the evidence that we had uncovered that proved the will was fraudulent. Attending the meeting were family members Katherine, Rebbie, Jackie, Janet, and Randy, five other probate attorneys, Brian Oxman (who was presenting the evidence), and myself. This meeting lasted approximately two hours. Brian Oxman did a superb job presenting all of the evidence that we had uncovered. He first showed us how the signatures were different. He then presented Michael's hotel bill to show that Michael was in New York from July 5th, to July 10th, 2002. He also presented evidence from interviews he had conducted with members of Michael's security where they stated that Michael did not sign a will on July 7th, 2002, while they were in New York. We all concluded after seeing additional pieces of evidence that the will is fraudulent and a fake.

John Branca is a lawyer, licensed to practice law in the State of California. This privilege subjects him to the Rules of Professional Responsibility of the State Bar of California. There are certain things that a lawyer is prohibited from doing. One of the prohibited activities is a breach of fiduciary duty which occurs when a lawyer uses his position to steal from a client.

Keeping in mind the foregoing, let's add another fact for your consideration. Sometime in February 2003, Michael Jackson fired John Branca. The first sentence of that letter states, "I am terminating the services of you and your firm...." Further in the letter, Michael Jackson states, "...you are commanded to immediately cease expending effort of any kind on my behalf...." Michael continued, "you are further demanded to execute any and all documents reasonably required of you...to transfer control over any and all files of mine (or any business of mine)...." Additionally, Michael Jackson said, "You are to deliver the original of all such documents to Mr. LeGrand, immediately...." Michael Jackson made the foregoing statements to Attorney John Branca in order to "have an immediate and orderly termination of your services...."

Now the very first thing that comes to mind is that if Michael Jackson ordered Branca to turn over all original documents, why did Branca not turn over the original "Last Will of Michael Joseph Jackson," along with the Michael Jackson Family Trust, that he was required and demanded to turn over to Michael's new attorneys?

The second thing that we need to focus on is that John Branca, as noted above, was allegedly fired by Michael Jackson because he breached his fiduciary duty to Michael by wrongfully inserting himself into the documents and contracts that addressed Michael Jackson's publishing catalogue without Michael's knowledge or authorization.

After Michael became informed of this despicable act by Branca, Michael fired him but not before Michael had to pay John Branca another $15 million dollars to recoup something that was already his. And to settle potential claims and lawsuits that surely would have emerged, if Michael Jackson was forced to sue John Branca to remove him from those contracts and documents.

The "Last Will and Testament of Michael Joseph Jackson" is alleged to have been executed on July 7th, 2002. However, the evidence shows that Michael Jackson was not even in Los Angeles on July 7th, 2002, because he was in New York City with the Reverend Al Sharpton protesting the actions and conduct of Tommy Mottola and Sony Records.

Another aspect of the so-called will is the fact that none of the witnesses have been made known publicly. Now, the whole purpose of having a witness (and in this case there were three witnesses), is to come forward and acknowledge that Michael Jackson was there with them at the time and on the day that this document was executed. Not a single one of the witnesses has come forth.

What still bothers me is that on several occasions, Michael Jackson told me that he never wanted to do business ever again with John Branca, Frank DiLeo, or Dr. Tohme Tohme. And now when I see John Branca, a man who Michael had grown to distrust, reigning over all of Michael Jackson's property, estate, and business holdings, it angers me to the highest degree. It is nothing short of one of the most despicable crimes that has ever happened in American history, that John Branca, a man who I believe stole from Michael Jackson and who breached his duties as a lawyer while working for Michael, is now sitting at the helm of the empire that Michael Jackson built.

In the discussions that I had with the lawyers at Janet Jackson's home, all of whom are noted specialists in the field of wills, trusts, and estates, I learned a few things about what makes a will legitimate. One of the primary requirements is for at least two witnesses to attest to the competency of the person making the will. In addition they are able to note whether the person is under duress, or the victim of fraud or undue influence. The witnesses can also assure that the will is being executed of his, or her, own free will. If an issue comes up on any of these matters, then the witnesses are supposed to be available for the court to determine if the will was freely executed and the person who made the will was not the victim of fraud or other misdeeds. But in Michael Jackson's case, the will that was shown to the public omits both the names and addresses of the witnesses. And there is no indication that the witnesses have ever been called into court under oath to testify to the truth of the so-called execution of the Michael Jackson will.

Another matter that bothers me tremendously is, that the judge in the Probate Court matter handling the Estate of Michael Jackson, made a ruling that Joe Jackson, Michael's father, did not have standing to challenge the legality of the so-called will. Now, just stop and think for a second, ladies and gentlemen, if Barbra Streisand had passed and someone outside of her family presented a will that left her entire estate in the hands and under the control of someone that is not a member of her family, and, let's say, Barbra Streisand's father or mother petitions the Probate Court to intervene and challenge the legality of the will, do you think that the court would tell them that they had no standing? It is both ludicrous and absurd. Fortunately, Joe Jackson and his attorney, Brian Oxman, are challenging this absurd decision on appeal where we hope that a panel of appellate court judges are not under the influence of John Branca as the Probate Court judge, in my opinion, clearly seems to be.

The public would like to know who these witnesses are and where they are located. For some reason, this is being kept a secret. We would like for these witnesses to come forward and admit under oath that they actually witnessed the signing of this will. We obviously know that if they put their signatures down on a legal document that is being used to defraud the Courts of the State of California this would be a very serious crime, punishable by imprisonment. John Branca knows this and so does John McClain.

I believe the Probate Court is a friend and confidante of John Branca, and they are doing all in their power to keep a lid on this powder keg issue. If the truth comes out that one, two, or all three of the witnesses knew that they were participating in a "fraud upon the court" in conjunction with John Branca, John McClain, and AEG, they would probably be seeking a way to get immunity from prosecution in exchange for their testimony which would implicate the remaining guilty parties in this tragic hoax.

For instance, wouldn't you want to know why these witnesses would claim to have witnessed Michael Jackson sign a will in Los Angeles? Especially when the evidence conclusively shows that Michael Jackson was in New York on the date and at the time John Branca claims that the will was executed? Secondly, you will recall that Michael Jackson fired John Branca at the same time that he fired Barry Siegel. Now Barry Siegel did the right thing and refused to participate in this fraud upon the court regarding Michael Jackson's estate. And in the letter that fired John Branca, Michael Jackson made it clear that Branca was not to be involved in any of Michael's business or personal dealings and affairs. There is no way that Michael Jackson would approve of John Branca being in total control of his estate.

Now while the legal challenge of Joe Jackson in the California Court of Appeals is continuing to play out, John Branca, John McClain, and AEG are draining the assets of the Michael Jackson Estate in my opinion. I truly believe the longer the officials in the State of California and the California components of the U.S. Department of Justice wait to take action against this gang of thieves, the longer it will take for Michael Jackson, his children, and his family to get the justice that they are entitled to. It is hard for me to believe as a life-long citizen of the United States that our government would sit by and allow this blatant, outright theft of Michael Jackson's estate to go without scrutiny and prosecution of those responsible.

On a final note, knowing Michael as I knew him, there is no way he would have ever stood for his final will and testament, to have the names of his children, misspelled. This was one of the main indicators, which I believe is further proof that the will is a total fake.

Michael Jackson Termination Letter to John Branca

Ziffren, Brittenham, Branca, Fischer,

Re: Discontinuance of Services

Dear John:

This is to confirm that I am terminating the services of you and your firm effective upon delivery of this letter. I have engaged David G. LeGrand, Esq., his firm, Hale Lane Peek Dennison & Howard , along with Booth Mitchel & Strange to represent my interests. I have also retained Paul Hastings and Janofsky to represent certain of my international interests. You are hereby requested to comply with the requests made of you and your firm in order to have an immediate and orderly termination of your services.

You are commanded to give Mr. LeGrand, Ms Brandt and their associates your full and unconditional cooperation. I have asked Mr. LeGrand and Ms. Brandt to obtain all of my files, records, documents, accounts for myself and all companies I own or control which may be in your possession. You are to deliver the originals of all such documents to Mr. LeGrand immediately. He will arrange copies to be returned to you.

You are commanded to immediately cease expending effort of any kind on my behalf, other than in direct cooperation with Mr. LeGrand and at his specific request. You are further directed to execute any and all documents reasonably required of you by Mr. LeGrand and Ms. Brandt to transfer control over any and all files of mine (or any business of mine) in accordance with their instructions.

I am also engaging the services of a new management company and you are to have no further discussion with Barry Siegel or Provident Financial Management with regard to my legal affairs. Mr. Siegel and Provident Financial Management no longer represent the interests of me or any business I own or control.

You are specifically instructed to immediately transfer any funds you are holding in trust for me to Mr. LeGrand.

I expect your full and complete cooperation with my new management company, Mr. LeGrand, Ms. Brandt or any other professionals under their direction to assist in their understanding my financial affairs, legal affairs and preparation of tax returns. You and your firm will be compensated at your ordinary and customary hourly rates for any such future assistance. Kindly deliver to Mr. LeGrand any invoice for your services through the date of this letter, when convenient.

Chapter Fifteen

Copy of The Actual Fraudulent Will

LAST WILL

OF

MICHAEL JOSEPH JACKSON

I, MICHAEL JOSEPH JACKSON, a resident of the State of California, declare this to be my last Will, and do hereby revoke all former wills and codicils made by me.

I

I declare that I am not married. My marriage to DEBORAH JEAN ROWE JACKSON has been dissolved. I have three children now living, PRINCE MICHAEL JACKSON, JR., PARIS MICHAEL KATHERINE JACKSON and PRINCE MICHAEL JOSEPH JACKSON, II. I have no other children, living or deceased.

II

It is my intention by this Will to dispose of all property which I am entitled to dispose of by will. I specifically refrain from exercising all powers of appointment that I may possess at the time of my death.

III

I give my entire estate to the Trustee or Trustees then acting under that certain Amended and Restated Declaration of Trust executed on March 22, 2002 by me as Trustee and Trustor which is called the MICHAEL JACKSON FAMILY TRUST, giving effect to any amendments thereto made prior to my death. All such assets shall be held, managed and distributed as a part of said Trust according to its terms and not as a separate testamentary trust.

If for any reason this gift is not operative or is invalid, or if the aforesaid Trust fails or has been revoked, I give my residuary estate to the Trustee or Trustees named to act in the MICHAEL JACKSON FAMILY TRUST, as Amended and Restated on March 22, 2002, and I direct said Trustee or Trustees to divide, administer, hold and distribute the trust estate pursuant to the provisions of said Trust, as hereinabove referred to as such provisions now exist to the same extent and in the same manner as though that certain Amended and Restated Declaration of Trust, were herein set forth in full, but without giving effect to any subsequent amendments after the date of this Will. The Trustee, Trustees, or any successor Trustees named in such Trust Agreement shall serve without bond.

IV

I direct that all federal estate taxes and state inheritance or succession taxes payable upon or resulting from or by reason of my death (herein "Death Taxes") attributable to property which is part of the trust estate of the MICHAEL JACKSON FAMILY TRUST, including property which passes to said trust from my probate estate shall be paid by the Trustee of said trust in accordance with its terms. Death Taxes attributable to property passing outside this Will, other than property constituting the trust estate of the trust mentioned in the preceding sentence, shall be charged against the taker of said property.

V

I appoint JOHN BRANCA, JOHN McCLAIN and BARRY SIEGEL as co-Executors of this Will. In the event of any of their deaths, resignations, inability, failure or refusal to serve or continue to serve as a co-Executor, the other shall serve and no replacement need be named. The co-Executors serving at any time after my death may name one or more replacements to serve in the event that none of the three named individuals is willing or able to serve at any time.

The term "my executors" as used in this Will shall include any duly acting personal representative or representatives of my estate. No individual acting as such need post a bond.

I hereby give to my Executors, full power and authority at any time or times to sell, lease, mortgage, pledge, exchange or otherwise dispose of the property, whether real or personal comprising my estate, upon such terms as my Executors shall deem best, to continue any business enterprises, to purchase assets from my estate, to continue in force and

Page 2

pay insurance premiums on any insurance policy, including life insurance, owned by my estate, and for any of the foregoing purposes to make, execute and deliver any and all deeds, contracts, mortgages, bills of sale or other instruments necessary or desirable therefor. In addition, I give to my Executors full power to invest and reinvest the estate funds and assets in any kind of property, real, personal or mixed, and every kind of investment, specifically including, but not by way of limitation, corporate obligations of every kind and stocks, preferred or common, and interests in investment trusts and shares in investment companies, and any common trust fund administered by any corporate executor hereunder, which men of prudent discretion and intelligence acquire for their own account.

VI

Except as otherwise provided in this Will or in the Trust referred to in Article III hereof, I have intentionally omitted to provide for my heirs. I have intentionally omitted to provide for my former wife, DEBORAH JEAN ROWE JACKSON.

VII

If at the time of my death I own or have an interest in property located outside of the State of California requiring ancillary administration, I appoint my domiciliary Executors as ancillary Executors for such property. I give to said domiciliary Executors the following additional powers, rights and privileges to be exercised in their sole and absolute discretion, with reference to such property: to cause such ancillary administration to be commenced, carried on and completed; to determine what assets, if any, are to be sold by the ancillary Executors; to pay directly or to advance funds from the California estate to the ancillary Executors for the payment of all claims, taxes, costs and administration expenses, including compensation of the ancillary Executors and attorneys' fees incurred by reason of the ownership of such property and by such ancillary administration; and upon completion of such ancillary administration, I authorize and direct the ancillary Executors to distribute, transfer and deliver the residue of such property to the domiciliary Executors herein, to be distributed by them under the terms of this Will, it being my intention that my entire estate

Page 3

shall be administered as a unit and that my domiciliary Executors shall supervise and control, so far as permissible by local law, any ancillary administration proceedings deemed necessary in the settlement of my estate.

VIII

If any of my children are minors at the time of my death, I nominate my mother, KATHERINE JACKSON as guardian of the persons and estates of such minor children. If KATHERINE JACKSON fails to survive me, or is unable or unwilling to act as guardian, I nominate DIANA ROSS as guardian of the persons and estates of such minor children.

I subscribe my name to this Will this ___ day of _____, 2002.

_____
MICHAEL JOSEPH JACKSON

On the date written below, MICHAEL JOSEPH JACKSON, declared to us, the undersigned, that the foregoing instrument consisting of five (5) pages, including the page signed by us as witnesses, was his Will and requested us to act as witnesses to it. He thereupon signed this Will in our presence, all of us being present at the same time. We now, at his request, in his presence and in the presence of each other, subscribe our names as witnesses.

Each of us is now more than eighteen (18) years of age and a competent witness and resides at the address set forth after his name.

Each of us is acquainted with MICHAEL JOSEPH JACKSON. At this time, he is over the age of eighteen (18) years and, to the best of our knowledge, he is of sound mind and is not acting under duress, menace, fraud, misrepresentation or undue influence.

Page 4

We declare under penalty of perjury that the foregoing is true and correct.

Executed on ~July 7th~ , 2002 at ~5:00 pm~ , ~Los Angeles, CA~

_____ Residing At ████████████████████

_____ Residing At ████████████████████

_____ Residing At ████████████████████

Estate of Michael Joseph Jackson
Petition for Probate of Will
Attachment 3e

The addresses of the witnesses to the execution of the Will have
been redacted in order to secure the safety and protect the
privacy of the witnesses.

Barry Siegel, CPA
Provident Financial Management

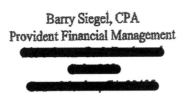

August 26, 2003

Mr. Michael Jackson
John G. Branca, Esq.
Mr. John McClain

Re: Michael Jackson Insurance Trust
     Michael Jackson Family Trust
     <u>Last Will of Michael Joseph Jackson</u>

Gentlemen:

The undersigned hereby acknowledges his previous resignation as a co-trustee of the Michael Jackson Insurance Trust.

The undersigned hereby advises you that he declines to act as a co-trustee of the Michael Jackson Family Trust and as a co-executor of the last will of Michael Joseph Jackson.

Very truly yours,

Barry Siegel

CONCLUSION

Conclusion

Over the years that I have known Michael Jackson, there have been many words that have been associated with him: awesome, incredibly talented, fantastic, and "The King of Pop", just to name a few. But did anyone ever stop to notice the humiliation and the pain he experienced at the expense of the media? In his later years, the pain that he felt was unbearable at times. Terms like "Wacko Jacko" and others tore him to pieces. I know it hurt him so much because Michael truly was more human than you or I could ever be. He was not a violent human being, nor was he a vindictive human being. However, with all of the fame and fortune he received during his lifetime, he was still a humble human being. Shortly after Michael died, his father, Joe Jackson said something to the world that I will never forget. What he said was that, "my son loved everybody". This was so true. Even those that wronged him, Michael always forgave them. I firmly believe that Michael's death was one of the greatest criminal injustices ever committed.

The only thing I ever hoped to accomplish by writing this book was to find justice for Michael. He was not only loved, but he was also adored around the world by millions. Not many artists have had the ability to make people weep just by their mere presence. Michael was one of those.

The world has been robbed of a great talent. Michael was more than a musical legend. He was one of God's special children. I once said to him, "there's no way you could have accomplished the things you have accomplished, or reach the heights that you have reached without the presence of Almighty God". His eyes begin to water and he then softly said, "I know. I am so grateful."

The only thing we have left to hold onto is his music and a few memories that I hope will never fade. His laughter and his playfulness will always be in my heart. But the feel of his presence is something I will always long for, and so will the millions of fans, that followed him faithfully throughout his entire career.

I'll never forget a conversation I had with Michael in Miami. He told me that he would never allow his children to watch television because of the terrible things they said about him in the media. I'll never forget the expression on his face when he said, "They never talk about the good things that I've done." So let me speak of them here for the record. Michael was not only an incredible songwriter, he was also an incredible vocalist, choreographer and dancer. Michael was also a true humanitarian. More times than any other entertainer, he was inducted into twelve Halls of Fame. He won fifteen Grammy Awards, twenty-six American Music Awards, received the Living Legend Award, and is in the Guinness Book of World Records. For four decades, Michael's music transcended generations and cultures around the world. In 1992, he founded "Heal the World," an organization that sent millions of dollars around the world to support children that were victims of disease, poverty, and violence. He was also a strong advocate for the prevention and awareness of HIV/AIDS. He helped draw attention to this deadly disease by publicly standing with the Clinton Administration to give more money to HIV charities and research programs. It is a shame that a man who literally loved and gave so much to the world died a victim of greed at the hands of a few.

In my opinion, the ultimate mistake committed by Michael was his trusting the wrong people in the entertainment industry. I feel that people such as John Branca, Randy Phillips, and Dr.

Conclusion

Tohme Tohme set out to take advantage of Michael at a time when he was the most vulnerable. They truly could have helped Michael, but what I saw did not reveal that. Michael told me personally that he did not agree to do fifty shows. He said he only agreed to do ten. Randy Phillips of AEG insists that Michael agreed to do fifty. With all of the lawyers at Randy Phillips disposal, he has yet to come forth with a signed contract showing that Michael agreed to fifty shows. He never produced such a contract and I truly believe he never will.

Michael did sign a contract hiring me to handle his business affairs and to oversee his finances for the tour in London. Michael always knew, from our early years together, that I would always have his best interests at heart. But Randy Phillips and Frank DiLeo did not want me around. They didn't want anyone around who would diminish their influence over Michael, and any person that they did not control. In my opinion, Randy Phillips wanted to maintain free reign over Michael so he would have no other choice but to do what they wanted him to do without interference. To try to make sure that I was out of the picture, I truly believe that Randy Phillips manufactured a highly publicized and phony letter, which I never received, claiming that Michael had terminated my contract. Michael told me himself that Randy Phillips had called him to his office for a meeting without telling him the nature of it. Michael said when he arrived, Randy Phillips told him that he must get rid of Leonard Rowe and that he was bringing in Frank DiLeo to manage him. And Michael said that Randy threatened him and told him that if he refused to do so that he would pull the plug on everything and demand payment on all of his advances immediately. I want you to remember that the despicable binding contract between AEG and Michael gave Randy Phillips the right to do this. But Michael still refused to get rid of me. Shortly after that is when Michael signed my agreement with him. None of this matters now; I never had the chance to protect Michael because he died.

When I heard the news of Michael's passing, I cried. I wished I had been in a position to do more to help him. I wish I had been able to remove the greedy and evil people from his life who didn't really care about his well-being. I wish I could have done more. But, I couldn't. They didn't want me, or anyone else that they did not control around Michael. I truly feel we would have interfered with their evil plans.

The ultimate display of injustice to Michael is that his legacy is not controlled by his family or his children as he would have intended it to be. Instead, it's going to the very people who I believe used him and also destroyed him. John Branca, the very same person who Michael personally told me that he would never do business with again, is controlling Michael's entire estate. The beneficiary of Michael's life insurance policy is not his mother and is not his children, but is AEG. How can this be? Michael's children are receiving $20,000 per month each, while John Branca and his cronies are paying themselves millions of dollars. But yet they refuse to give Joe Jackson, Michael's father, anything. I ask this question, would Michael have decided to do this, depriving his dearly beloved children and his family? The answer is simple. He did not, and he would not.

Just like what I believe to be a phony termination letter that they are saying Michael signed and sent to me, I also believe that the Last Will and Testament presented to the court by John Branca and John McClain (conveniently listing them as executors for his estate) is also fraudulent and phony. The will gives John Branca, Michael's former attorney whom Michael accused of embezzling from him, control of his entire estate.

Shortly after Michael died, the executives at Sony Music Entertainment signed a record-breaking deal worth $250 million with Michael's estate, in which John Branca is now the executor. The question I cannot shake is why are these people getting away with the wrongs they are doing to Michael's children and his family? How can we as Americans allow them to get away with this?

In my opinion, John Branca, Randy Phillips, and AEG had no interest in ever trying to restore Michael Jackson's physical or financial condition. I truly feel they only wanted to strip the superstar of his worldly possessions which include his priceless music catalogue, and to enjoy and share in the wealth that Michael's name and his brand would surely bring for years and years to come. The only way this could have ever been accomplished was that Michael Jackson had to die.

From me to you, Mike,

I love you, Michael. You will always be in my heart. May God continue to be with you and bless you as he did during your stay, here on Earth. I thank you so much for all you have done for me. I will hold on to the memories that you have given me forever.

Leonard Rowe